RUDY'S DOGHOUSE

RUDY'S DOGHOUSE

MEMORIES OF MY CHILDHOOD

JUDITH VILLEMAIN

COPYRIGHT

Copyright © 2019 by Judith Villemain
All rights reserved.

Published by Fifth Estate Media
Cover art by J. Susan Cole Stone
Copyediting by Laureen Crowley

No part of this book may be reproduced in any form or by any electronic or mechanical means, including information storage and retrieval systems, without written permission from the author, except for the use of brief quotations in a book review.

For my Family

CHAPTERS

1. Meet James, Birth
2. Punishment Lineup, Age three to twelve
3. Building Toys, Age three to twelve
4. Rudy's Doghouse, Age four
5. Rudy the Runaway, Age four
6. Running Away Again, Age four
7. This is Love, Age four
8. Shells, Age four to twelve
9. Contrast, Age four to twelve
10. I am Stupid, Age four to twenty-three
11. Magic Vase, Age five
12. Despairing Pool, Age five
13. Puzzled Love, Age five
14. Christmas Tree Birthday, Age five
15. Rudy's Stuffed Kitty-cat, Age six
16. Rain Prayer, Age six
17. Secret Contract, Age six
18. Goofy, Age Six

19. Starving Musicians, Age six
20. Chrissie Evert Perfection, Age six
21. Rudy's Halloween, Age six
22. Nurse Rudy, Age seven
23. Outlaw Leader, Age seven
24. Toys for Boys, Age seven
25. Beach Summer, Age seven
26. College Mom, Age eight
27. Calico Drive-Over, Age eight
28. First Diet, Age nine
29. Snow White, Age ten
30. What is Love, Age twelve
31. The Mountain House, Age twelve to eighteen
32. Beans and Rice, Age twelve to eighteen
33. Driving Lessons, Age twelve to sixteen
34. Family Ice Cream, Age twelve to fourteen
35. Burning Time, Age twelve to fourteen
36. Kitty-cats on the Roof, Age twelve
37. The Motorcycle, Age twelve
38. Pansy Face Garden, Age twelve
39. Love Burns, Age twelve
40. My Plan, Age thirteen to twenty-three
41. Beloved Patient, Age thirteen
42. Hopeless Determination, Age thirteen
43. Tarzan and Jane, Age thirteen
44. Begging for Wishes, Age fourteen
45. Boarding School Friends, Age fifteen
46. Around the Country, Age sixteen
47. Whore, Age eighteen
48. The White Cabinet, Age twenty-three
49. Dad's Final Peace, Age thirty-one to thirty-three

50. Dad's Presence, Age thirty-four
51. Help, Age thirty-five
52. After Help, Age thirty-five
53. Mom, Age thirty-seven
54. You Are Extraordinary, Age fifty

Appendix
    I: Rudy's Activities
    II: Rudy's Home Rules from Memory
    III: Rudy's Church Rules from Memory

INTRODUCTION

Rudy's Doghouse is meant to be a story that relates to people who believe they have been victims in life, who have been abused, and/or who have been disregarded.

    I am telling my story to let you know that I have walked in some of the shadows and darkness of life. I have experienced some of life's disappointments. But we don't have to wallow in place, experiencing the familiar pain and unworthiness. We can move forward; we can each take our lives and make them better, a little bit at a time. And suddenly, after some time, a miracle happens; and we are different. We are proud of ourselves. Let this be an inspiration to you or one of your friends. May it bring you support, love, hope, and happy wishes.

PERSONAL STATEMENT

The names have been changed in order to protect the parties involved. This is the way I remember my past to the best of my knowledge. These are my personal memories. My mother remembers these stories that I have told and knows them to be true to her memories as well.

Some of the material in this book may be sensitive or offensive, particularly to children. Please use caution and judgment.

FOREWORD

My whole goal is to try to reach out to you – to try and make a connection. If you are like me, you want to be left alone. You can deal with this alone. You don't need help. Or do you? I'm hoping that you can relate to my story, and that by seeing my movement toward the light and happiness in this life, maybe, just maybe, you can start to find your own.

1

AGE BIRTH

MEET JAMES

Several weeks before Mom's due date, which was January 19th, Mom was at home by herself. She started having contractions unexpectedly and they rushed her to the hospital. As soon as Mom was situated in the labor room, Dad called his buddies with the good news that his second son was going to be born that night, so they decided to celebrate at their favorite restaurant. Dad had another baby boy on the way. Dad had been married before and had a three-year old son, my older brother.

Mom was at the hospital in the delivery room. She was having difficulties and the doctors decided to perform a C-section to deliver the baby. They prepared her and began the procedure. Soon I was born. But there was a big surprise; I was not a boy, I was a girl. Mom was happy, but Dad was not. I was healthy, and everything went well with the delivery.

When the nurse came around to fill in the paperwork, she asked Mom what my name was going to be. My Mom replied, "It was going to be James." There was no planned named for a baby girl. They would have to think about it.

Dad was disappointed, but he was glad I was a healthy baby and very beautiful. Mom and Dad thought about my name for three days before deciding the best one for me: Rudy.

2

AGE: THREE THROUGH TWELVE

THE PUNISHMENT LINEUP

Daddy punished us about three times in a typical week. Even if the house and yard were clean and in perfect shape, Daddy would still make up a reason to punish us. He was never happy with what we did. I think that when we were especially good, it made him even more angry. We really couldn't win, no matter how hard we always tried.

Our punishment lineup was: three children in a line, biggest to smallest, oldest child whipped first, middle child whipped second, youngest child whipped third, and the "deed-doer" whipped last, sometimes with the buckle-side of the belt.

Dad lined us up in a row in the middle of our family room, which was where Daddy's chair was located. We called his chair "Daddy's Throne." No one could sit in that chair except Daddy. Daddy was king of our home. King over us. King over Mom. And I used to think he wanted to be king over the world.

As we lined up, our toes were in a row. Our order was left to right, and after a little space, stood Mom. She stood on our side of the room. I had never realized that before. But there she stood in her place. She never stood with Daddy or even walked over to his side of the room when we were being punished. She was always silent, still, and vanishingly present. I always wondered if Mom was going to be the next one to be punished; I felt as if she was one of us kids.

Daddy had his belt in hand. It was folded over and he was snapping it, putting dread and desperation in our minds. It scared us to death. Not only was he furious with us, he was furious with the world too. His face grew red; and an evil and monstrous force grew from within him.

Without hesitation my older brother stepped forward, turned, dropped his pjs and bent over into position, closing his eyes, waiting for that dreaded moment. If he had not stepped forward, things would have gotten worse. He did what he was supposed to do. Daddy would beat him until he cried, so it usually took a bit of time. He didn't want to cry, but it always ended up that he did; he could not help but cry. He usually ended up on his knees by the time it was over. He would have to get himself together and get up off the floor and back in line as efficiently as possible. By this time, my little sister and I had tears running down our faces in a silent resolve.

Then it was my turn; I stepped forward and took the position in front of him, turning to the side. We knew how it worked. We knew that Daddy could get worse. We tried to ease the process best we could. Daddy belted me from my neck all the way down to my ankles. The belt had a severe stinging effect. The lash-marks on my body lasted three or four days depending on Daddy's mood. Luckily there was no buckle on this particular day.

Then it was my little sister's turn. She was so small. She took the position. Daddy lifted her up with one hand by the arm, hanging her in the air like a delicate glass ornament. And then he started thrashing her, over and over. She trembled and swung through the air back and forth. I waited for her to fall and hit the ground breaking into a million tiny pieces. We could not comfort each other. And we dared not look at each other.

To finish off our punishment cycle, the "deed-doer" would step forward for an additional beating. If no one stepped forward, Daddy punished all of us again. So, the rule was to figure out beforehand, if we could, who was going to take the blame.

The "deed-doer" would then step forward and take a whipping that was harder and longer than all the others. Most of the time, this involved the belt-buckle side. It usually put us out of commission for the rest of the day. Bruising was a definite. Sometimes, but not always, there was blood.

After we received our punishment, we marched out of the room single file and headed to our rooms. That was the rule. We were to go there and stay there until and if we were called. We lay on our beds. We could not read books. We had to stay quiet. When I received this last part of the punishment, I usually lay in a ball in my bed until the next day.

Soothing Damages

I know that when my brother received the last part of the punishment, he would get angry. And when he returned to his room, he would throw things and break them. I could hear them breaking. And Mom and Dad would then yell at him.

I think my father was raised similarly; I think this is all he knew. He was a former medical officer in the Navy. I think the two came together for him and made sense somehow. He never made the adult decisions to change any of his ways; maybe he didn't know that he could. He was constantly fighting somebody or something, and probably wasn't aware of it.

His parents were divorced. He was raised by his elderly mother and two older sisters. His sisters never married, and they ruled his life completely. He said many times that he could never make them happy. He was brilliant in his studies. He received a scholarship in music to Julliard, but his oldest sister insisted that he major in medicine. He did what he was told and graduated in the top ten in his class.

~

3

AGE: THREE THROUGH TWELVE

Building Toys

We worshipped on the seventh day of the week. So, on Sabbath, we usually entertained people from church, or we visited friends for the afternoon. It was usually a big event, and everyone was tired when we were done for the day.

I remember Daddy in the kitchen on those days; otherwise, he was never in the kitchen. But when we had guests, he washed dishes and I usually helped him.

Our friends would compliment Daddy and how he helped in the kitchen. He was happy to do dishes on these days.

Occasionally, Dad would have a good day and one of the things we would do together was construct with building toys at home. We had a closet full of them, near the family room. Mostly we had building blocks, but we had building logs, and sticks and wheels too.

Dad liked for us to play with toys that made us use our brains.

We created piles of blocks on the family room floor in a wide circle. My brother and I would follow Daddy's lead. We had several boards that served as the base for these projects. Daddy would arrange them and tell us the plan for the day. And then we would build.

One block at a time; one task at a time. We created designs that taught us about architectural and bridge structures.

Sometimes we tried to create animals, or we built a landscape of buildings creating a skyline. One of the things he taught us was that if we made a mistake, we could always undo the blocks and start over. We sometimes would play for three or four hours at a time. It was great fun and quality time with Dad. He seemed to be happy and we worked hard to please him.

When we went to Uncle Mark's house for the day, he had an odd-shaped building toy that we played with on Sabbath. And Daddy and Uncle Mark would play with those too.

We built massive structures with these for hours. My aunt frowned about the whole thing wondering if we should be doing that on Sabbath or not.

But the men ruled, so we won out on that account.

Soothing Damages

These are some of my happiest memories. Time with my father was valuable and very rare. We didn't talk a lot. But just being with him and working on a project together was dear to me. It was times like this that permitted me to see my father in a loving manner.

One of the things I find interesting to point out is that my education is in architecture. I wonder now if that comes from these fleeting moments of happiness and love that I experienced with my father, building with architecture toys. Perhaps I was reaching out for those emotions once more.

4

AGE: FOUR

Rudy's Doghouse

I was staring out through the glistening spiderwebs at Pooch; I called to him to join me in the shabby wooden doghouse where I had taken refuge. Raindrops fell through the holes in the roof onto my skin and goosebumps appeared. My face was completely wet by now and I was cold. The sun was going to set soon, and I was afraid of the dark. Then Pooch came bounding in, shaking all his wetness over me and then turning around and around before snuggling down with me. At least he didn't smell too bad. I was warm enough now, with my beloved dog, who listened to everything I ever had to say... and didn't say. I felt that he could read my thoughts. He knew when I was unhappy and when something was wrong. He had his way of letting me know that he cared.

He was a gray and white schnauzer. As soon as he saw

one of us, he would wag his tail. He was a happy dog, very smart and intuitive.

When Daddy came home late that evening, we all ran from the room before he came in the door – that was usual... hiding in our rooms – hoping everything was going to be perfect. Was it? Inevitably, he would yell for us to line up. Something was wrong with that tone of voice... terribly wrong. We lined up in a hurry, making sure we had each hair in place, were in the right positions and all our toes were lined up with each other. I was usually wide-eyed, waiting, unknowing what was coming and afraid. This particular night was no different.

The customary interviewing took place. As always, we were showered and in our pajamas before Daddy came home. This time there was a problem with the towels. They were not evenly lined up. We each took our usual punishment. Then, instead of the "wrong doers" turn or the second round of punishment, he decided instead to sentence me to go to bed hungry and sleep alone outside. I would rather have gotten beaten. But I didn't dare ever speak back to Daddy, not ever.

So obediently, I went out into the weedy, little backyard in my pajamas with my bare feet in the sandy dirt. I didn't want to sleep on the cold wet ground, so that's how I ended up in the doghouse. It was still lightly raining and it was a little cold. Pooch was pretty much my bud and my dog. He never had enough trims. He was the sweetest animal. He was terribly mistreated by Daddy, but the rest of the family loved him. He was our little protector.

Predictably enough, I was terrified that night. I remember looking up through the slats of wood on the roof of the doghouse and seeing shadows moving over us, big shadows, moving back and forth. And the spiders just got bigger and bigger as the night got longer and longer. I huddled with Pooch, shaking with fear and shaking from the goosebumps that appeared on my skin.

I must have dozed here and there, because I made it through the night. I was still damp in the morning. Pooch and I crawled out of the doghouse looking truly sad, I imagine. I tried the screen door to the house, but it was locked, so I peed in the bushes along the big fence in the back. No one must be up yet. So, I sat with Pooch for a while waiting to be let inside to start another day.

Soothing Damages
That doghouse and I knew each other well enough. And my brother and younger sister knew it as well. My brother tried to keep the wood nailed onto the frame; he knew the meaning of having the doghouse as a refuge from the night. Later, when we were older, my sister would open the window in our room on the end of the house and hand out a piece of bread that she had stolen from the dinner table for me. If she had been caught, it would have been the end of her. I suppose I visited that tattered doghouse until I was twelve and we moved to North Carolina.

Chapter 4

5

AGE: FOUR

RUDY THE RUNAWAY

My little suitcase was an old one given to me by my dad. His name was spelled out on it with black letters across the hard green and white surface. But I liked it because it was little like me. Pulling on my red velveteen coat, I ran one hand over the soft material and then tied the belt.

Mom had yelled at me. Mom was usually nice to me. If Mom and Daddy were both going to yell at me, then I was done. Tears streamed down my face and onto my hand as I packed Obey, my stuffed owl. I couldn't live here anymore; I just couldn't bear it anymore. Mom and Dad were gone. My brother and sister weren't home. Just the babysitter was around cleaning the house. But I knew I could sneak past her. This was my chance.

Chapter 5

In my room, I packed carefully and quietly. My baby boy doll was placed carefully in there, along with his extra diaper, a blue bottle, and my soft blanket. That took up most of the room. I packed several polished rocks that fit in the palm of my hand. They flaunted a little shiny pink pull-string bag. And I added a couple of chocolate-chip pecan cookies that I had stolen from the kitchen. I closed my suitcase and pushed the latches tight until I heard them click. I slid my little hand through the clear plastic handle of the case and pulled it off the floor. I was ready.

I peered outside my bedroom door and saw no one. Everyone had gone to work or school. I was four, so I hadn't started school yet. Down the hall I soundlessly marched, first through the living room, then through a second long hall at the end. I didn't run into my babysitter. Whew. Onto the utility room and out the door into the garage. The garage door opened when I pushed the button. I walked to the very edge of the floor in the garage, just before the driveway concrete. My toes on the line. I looked up and breathed in the morning air; it was crisp. Was I sure about this? I wondered. Staring, soon glazed over, at the tree tops and sky. Time passed.

The door opened behind me. I did not turn. It would be the babysitter. She came and stood beside me, silent, and crossed her arms, sighing. We both just stared out into the nothingness that was there.

"So, what did you pack?" she finally asked, disturbing the quiet.

Making a frown, I plopped down and opened my suitcase.

"Walking, you won't make it very far," she said matter-offactly. "And you will need money," as she examined the contents of my suitcase.

Slowly, I put my precious items back into the case. She was right. I had no big plan. No money. No place to go. If I was going to leave home, it was going to need to be done with much thought and careful planning.

Soothing Damages
My brother had run away many times throughout his childhood. He always ended up coming back home within a few days or maybe a bit longer. My little sister ran away from home too after she was 18 years of age. She was successful when some friends of hers let her live with them for three months. Ultimately, she came home though. I learned from them too. I learned that the plan had to be real, safe, resilient, and permanent.

6

AGE: FOUR

Running Away Again

May put my lunch on the counter and lifted me up on the bar stool. She told me to eat my lunch. She left me there to go to a different part of the house to finish cleaning. I quickly finished eating and called for May to help me off the bar stool, because it was too tall for me to get off by myself. But she didn't hear me.

As I was waiting for her to return, I discovered that I could swing the chair part of the stool back and forth. So then, I decided to find out what would happen if I stood up on the bar stool and tried to swing it back and forth. I balanced myself by hanging on to the edge of counter in front of me.

My mom returned home just in time to see me rotating the chair to the left and right, standing up on it. She did not like what she saw, and she yelled at me to sit down immediately. Mom didn't yell at me; only Daddy yelled at me. I was heartbroken. I could not understand why this was happening to me. Now, both of my parents were yelling at me.

I waited for my brother to get home and confided in him. He told me Mom doesn't yell about things more than once. And that if she did yell at me, it had to be very important. But I wasn't buying it. Mom wasn't supposed to yell at me.

When I went to bed that night, I tossed and turned. I was not happy. I decided it was time to pack my little suitcase and leave home for real this time. So, the next day, when May was working in another part of the house, and everyone else was gone, I quietly packed. Snapping my suitcase shut, I crept out of the house by the front door. The warm humid air hit my face like a still wall and I felt the sun's hot rays.

I decided to turn left when I reached the main road. That would lead me out of the community. I had just come up to the small rock bridge when I spotted Mom's car coming, so I quickly darted into the bushes that were along the road. She didn't see me and passed by. I kept walking down the road toward my first goal, the community gate. I was sweating and thirsty for water by that point. But I wasn't going to let that stop me.

Mom arrived home and May left. May was driving down the road when she encountered me walking with my suitcase. It took some convincing, but May persuaded me once again that home was where I needed to stay. So, I jumped into her car and she drove me home. She took my hand and walked me to the front door of my home, ringing the doorbell. Mom answered the door and she could not believe who she saw standing there. She welcomed me back home. I asked Mom not to tell Daddy. Happily, she kept her part of the bargain.

7

AGE: FOUR

THIS IS LOVE

Regnad, who was several years older than me, explained to me that if we were going to be friends and love each other, that we needed to share a secret, a very special secret. I liked the idea, because he was mean to me a lot and this would require that he stop being mean and love me more. I agreed. He was much older than I. The big secret would be that we would pretend to be boyfriend and girlfriend and play house. We swore to each other not to tell another soul. It was just between us. And so, it was.

I would wait for him to get home from school and I would let him see my private area. Sometimes, he might even touch me there. But it was simple and childish. I thought it was okay. And it sealed the deal. It was worth it to me not to get hit or kicked or to be unloved anymore. I needed to be accepted. I needed to know that I was loved, and I looked forward to spending time with him.

A few times he wanted me to dress real pretty and stand in his driveway, so when he came home from school, he would be welcomed by me. He told me to wave at him like I was glad to see him. And he said he would tell all the boys at his school that he had a girlfriend. He was proud of me. He taught me about music on the radio, and just talked to me. It was nice. I had a warmth in my heart for him. During this time with him I could forget my problems. Or so I thought.

Reg made forts in the woods behind his house. One fort for each of us. I had to pull back the branches to enter my fort, but once inside it was quite spacious and had cross branches to sit on. These forts were great places to hide.

On occasion, Reg and I would meet in my fort or his fort and play house. I would of course agree to take on the wifely duties that go along with that. It all seemed innocent enough. Things were kept simple. But I had a gnawing feeling that something wasn't right.

Soothing Damages

This was the beginning of our relationship. The relationship grew more and more physical as I grew older each year. It felt good, and I thought it was OK. When he wanted to escalate the relationship to a sexual one, at age twelve, I wanted it all to stop. I explain more in Chapter 30.

8

AGE: FOUR TO TWELVE

Shells

I covered myself in sand; I had it in my hair, in my fingers and between my toes. I loved days on the beach with my family. We could run, play, swim, surf, and build sand castles. Running along the shoreline was one of my favorites, kicking up the watery sand and getting even dirtier. Then we would run into the ocean and clean the sand off, starting the process all over again.

Building sand castles was the most fun of the day. Mom would help us. She taught us how to drain a mixture of sand and water through our fist and let it drip onto the castle walls to make spirals and towers. We placed shells on the castle walls and on the castle. A large moat circled the castle walls and headed out to sea, filling and emptying the moat as the waves moved in and out. Our castle was built strong and lasted for hours, but Mother Nature always brought our

Chapter 8

castle down with the continual pounding of ocean waves. The next morning, we started over, having a blast.

Daddy would usually go for a walk and take us kids with him. Dad was happy being on the beach. We would walk the shoreline looking for shells. Sometimes we would run into the smaller whitecaps to catch rolling shells. Daddy's favorites were conchs, cat-eyes, screw shells, apples, sunbursts, Venuses, and sundials. We looked for those first, but we would pick up all kinds of shells for our buckets. I liked to pick out shells that were not perfect but had character. I found beauty in the odd fascinations. It was time with Dad. And it was fun.

Near the end of the day, part of the family tradition was to bring your bucket of shells to Dad and let him sift through it. He would line up the shells by hierarchy, from the best ones down to the holey, broken ones. He controlled which ones we could keep and which ones we had to leave on the beach. The special ones I had picked were thrown by the wayside. They were beautiful, and I got upset a few times about the whole ordeal, but I learned quickly that getting upset didn't help.

After soaking, washing and drying the shells, Daddy would have me arrange the shells in a big glass jar. He taught me how to strategically place the attractive shells, so they would be seen, and place the less interesting shells in the middle. I became efficient at decorating the glass jars.

Soothing Damages

When I was seven years old, my parents purchased a condominium on one of the beaches in Florida as we were spending more and more weekends there. My whole family enjoyed spending time there. We could relax and forget about the stresses of everyday life. I loved it there.
I still make shell jars to this day from shells we find on the beach. I give them as gifts to family and friends. I decorate my home with them. They are full of happy memories.
The castle was about enlightenment. I take away the fact that Mother Nature always wins. Time may heal all wounds, but there are scars left over to remind me of what has passed. Scars that I will forever carry.
As far as the shells my father didn't like, I had to learn that being special wasn't necessarily a worthy thing. Being perfect was the valuable thing.
Perfection was something my father insisted on. My instinct is still to search out perfection, and to be perfect. However, I also fight this tendency every day. Today, I believe everyone and everything has its place and time. Today I will pick up an imperfect shell because of its shiny inside, or a conch that has its tip broken off. And I will keep them and show them off in my shell jars.
Character is beauty.

9

AGE: FOUR TO TWELVE

Contrast

Whenever Daddy was at work during the days, our life at home with Mom was great. We treasured that time together. It was peaceful, and we got along well together. There was no yelling; there was music or humming a song. There was laughter sometimes.

We feared the time Daddy came home. And it was all shattered. As soon as we heard his car pulling into the driveway, we would grab our homework, or toys, and run for our lives. The moment he came through the door, everything became a war zone. He would usually be yelling or shouting hurtful words at us. Or he would entertain himself by pitting one of us against the other, manipulating the situation like a puppet master.

This always left Mom there alone to face Daddy's arrival home. She received the worst of him before he had a chance to calm down. Daddy usually came in the door yelling at Mom and sometimes abruptly pushing her aside. He would blame her for everything. I became concerned for her, but I was too scared to stand with her against Daddy. I watched from a safe hidden place sometimes. She never looked happy at these times, she had a look of disbelief in her eyes. She needed help, and I had no idea how to help her.

Soothing Damages

My mother had the best of intentions for all of us children. She was a medical secretary, but on her own would not have been able to support three children without my father's help. She had several chances to divorce my father, but when she found out that my father might get custody of us kids, she decided to stay for our sakes. She was a buffer of sorts, and someone who unconditionally loved us. Without her, I think we would have been lost. With her, we at least had a chance to make it in this world.

10

AGE: FOUR TO TWENTY THREE

I am Stupid

"Come here Stupid," my dad yelled. I came running. That was my name some of the time. When he was in a good mood it was Sugar. When he was in a bad mood, it was Stupid, or Dumb Dumb. My siblings and I all took our turns with these demoralizing names throughout our lives, which is strange because each of us was bright in our own respect. My brother, I think, was the smartest. I remember Dad saying that my brother was a board-certified genius, scoring IQ tests at a genius level. I think he rivaled my dad in smartness. My sister and I didn't do as well on the IQ exams as our brother, but we proved scholastically rigorous.

However, anytime we scored a B in classwork or on testing, our dad would let us know how disappointed he was in our abilities. Time and time again. Even into my master's degree at a prestigious private university, my dad raged that I could have done something better. It was never good enough. Even when I earned diplomas, my dad was somehow disappointed.

2ND GRADE

I was called stupid so many times in my life that I believed I was stupid. It was hard to believe I had a brain. It was only after I received my master's degree that I began to believe people's compliments. I was just ecstatic that I was finished with schooling and I had my ticket to freedom in my hand. I felt terrific. No longer would I be bound, forced and obligated to my old life. I was going to crawl out of this dark pit of insanity, even if it was all by myself. And I was going to find the sun shining on my face.

11

AGE: FIVE

The Magic Vase

Mom was frantic. She was all dressed up and had her purse in hand. She always looked so pretty to me. Perfect black hair with her dark eyes. And her little dresses that she made by hand were so graceful and detailed. Today she was wearing yellow, her favorite color.

"Rudy, have you seen my keys?" she asked in desperation.

No one else was home so it was up to us to find them, I decided. We went through each room on a mission: first the master bedroom by her purse area and even in the drawers, then the kitchen and kitchenette by the phone area, then the family room, and so on. We couldn't find the keys anywhere. We looked under couch cushions, behind silk flowers, over books and even in the fish tank. Where oh where could they be?

I knew I could find them. So, I told Mom to stay in the

family room and I would be right back. I ran to my room; and knelt by my bedside and prayed. "Please help me find the keys." And I had an instant vision in my head of a section of the marble vase that Daddy thought was so special. I could see inside the vase, and there were Mom's keys.

I ran to tell Mom in relief and confidence. Mom reached toward the marble vase on the fireplace mantel and opened it. She had to use two hands to bring it down. Sure enough, there were her keys.

Soothing Damages

After that, when small things disappeared, they began showing up in the marble vase. Watches, coins, keys, rings and sometimes odd things, like small rocks or little toy cars. So, I dubbed it the "Magic Vase." I think back on it now, and I think the vase had a mysterious helper.

12

AGE: FIVE

THE DESPAIRING POOL

I watched my brother being beaten through showering tears. My brother tried to be brave at first but as he was beaten, he wilted and ended up lying on the floor in a heap. I heard a stammering whisper, "Stop, you're going to kill him, stop!" My mom's voice got stronger as she repeated herself. Then in a state of suspended belief, I saw my mom's body move toward my dad. I was confused. She kept moving in that direction until she was between my brother's body and Daddy's swinging belt. He hit her two or three times before stopping. He had been in a rage. He looked stunned. He immediately stomped down the hallway and slammed the door to the master bedroom. We all just stood there in shock. Mom had her arms around my brother. He could barely stand up with her help.

She told us to go to our rooms. We would be relatively

safe back there. So, we ran off to our rooms. Mom took care of my brother.

The brutal scene started when Mom and Dad were getting ready to head off to an overseas vacation for two weeks. I remember being sad when they left us. Dad had made us promise not to clean out the pool too, which seemed weird.

As soon as my parents walked out the door, my older brother told me to grab a bucket. We were going to empty the pool bucket by bucket. Our babysitter didn't say anything either way. So, off we went while she watched my little sister.

I remember the small pool having an opaque nastiness; it was filled with dead leaves, mold, algae, dirt, mud, frogs, tadpoles, worms, and probably scary things. We emptied the pool slowly, inch by inch. I remember being about three quarters finished, carrying my bucket, walking down the pool stairs and onto the pool flooring. Then I went down the slope to the deep end where there was still muck and water. By now I was covered in mess, with mud on my face and in my hair. The sun was going down. We only had four days left before our parents were going to come back. It would take every minute working to get that pool emptied. We were exhausted.

We went inside and did our usual routines – showering, dinner, and bed.

And that's when it happened. I woke up to Daddy's voice yelling for my brother. The babysitter was grabbing her purse and running for the door. Dad and Mom had arrived home from their trip. As fate would have it, he immediately walked to the kitchen window and saw the disaster. I went to the window to join everyone else there just staring. And there it was. The entire pool had lifted out of the ground; broken concrete, twisted rebar, and a broken despairing heap remained.

I don't remember the sound of it rising out of the ground. I was sleeping that night along with the rest of the household. But you would think it would have been loud. Maybe I awoke, and went back to sleep not knowing what the noise was all about.

My brother and I held hands at the window. There was no need to say anything. We knew what was coming.

Soothing Damages
We must not have known about the faucet that empties pool water, or maybe it didn't work because the water was too contaminated with muck. Either way, buckets are what we used.
I remember thinking my brother was going to die by my father's hands. I also remember thinking that there was nothing I could do about it. I was in fear for my life, and the lives of my siblings and Mom too.
I remember wishing I would just die on several occasions. At that point in time, my whole life was built on and around fear.

13

AGE: FIVE

PUZZLED LOVE

With or without company on the Sabbath, we sometimes worked on puzzles, marvelous big ones with loads of pieces. One was of fireworks in the night sky. Others were of beautiful landscapes and nature. But the fireworks project stood out most for me. It had a black background, which was very unusual for our projects, and it had bursting balls of colored lights all over it. Mostly there were orange explosions, but there were rose and purple too. My favorite was the purple one.

Daddy was in charge, as always. We would put the straight, edge pieces down first on cardboard. Finding all the edges was the first challenge and we would go through the pieces three or four times to find the pattern. Then slowly we would work our way inwards, following the colors of light toward their centers. My dad, my brother and I were good at puzzles. And together we were a driven, focused team. The magic in those moments of time spun its way around our hearts and through our souls. There was a feeling of togetherness, which didn't happen often.

My dad could spot a piece from afar or close. My brother and I would work with our heads over the puzzle earnestly searching for the perfect fit. And when we found that right piece, we would grin and look up at our father, to meet another grin. Sometimes, Daddy would even say an encouraging word or two; we lived and breathed on the edge of that precipice.

It usually took us one or two weekends to finish a puzzle. I remember putting the last piece in the fireworks puzzle. I remember being sad about it. But I smiled. It was perfection and complete. The three of us were a team.

Soothing Damages
The part that confused me when I was a child was that I was loved during the puzzle project time. But when that time was finished, love seemed dark and void again. Love confused me. It was conditional. I had to be doing something right or perfect to receive that love. Dad's love did not come freely, nor did it come from the heart.
Now I look back and I think my father was in his element when doing puzzles. He was in charge, it was methodical, there was a sequence, there was progress, and there was an achievement. These things pleased him.
Perhaps having order in the middle of life's chaos was a relief for him. He carried a lot of stress and a lot of unsolved problems. He didn't like to talk about his life. Apparently, he had to fight his own battles.

14

AGE: FIVE

Christmas Tree Birthday

It was late Christmas Eve and we snuck out of our rooms and sure enough, Santa had come. The gifts were under the tree. We had our trusty flashlights and we went on our adventure. Our method of silliness was to open a tiny bit of the wrapping paper at the corner to get a clear look at the box. From that, we would guess what was in the box. We each usually received one gift. And then the three of us would get a group gift or sometimes two. After playing our guessing game and sneaking a few cookies, off to bed we crept, happy and knowing the next morning would be grand.

After a good breakfast at our little kitchen table, we cleaned up and ran to the living room still in our pjs for Christmas festivities. Christmas morning was splendid. We looked forward to this time. Daddy was usually in a decent mood on Christmas when I was young.

My older brother was first. He would open his gift. Then I would open mine. Mine was a baby boy doll that year. I was in love. He was the cutest little thing. My sister was always last to open her gifts. Then to finish our gifts up, we would open our group gift together. It was a little-people garage set with extra people and cars; it was so cool. We finished watching Mom and Dad swap gifts. And then we asked if we could go play with our slowly growing set of Little People village. We had a school, a house, a Ferris wheel and a garage.

Later that evening we came together again for dinner and then we sat under the Christmas tree again. It was time for my brother's birthday. His birthday was the same day as Christmas Day. He had two or three gifts under the tree that were new. I was always jealous of my brother's birthday display under the Christmas tree. The lights and the ornaments were so magical. An idea came to me, but I knew I had to time it right. So, I waited until we were finished celebrating my brother's birthday. And I thought, I would ask the question the next morning. So, during breakfast the next morning, I asked Mom if we could leave the Christmas tree up until my birthday. It was two weeks after my brother's birthday. I didn't see why we couldn't. Mom said she would talk to Dad and they would discuss it. That's the best I could hope for, so I left it alone.

I waited a day and a half for them to speak about my proposal. And at our meeting in the family room, where we each sat in assigned chairs, Daddy announced that I would be allowed to have the Christmas tree up for my birthday. There were two conditions: that all the other Christmas decorations would be put away, and that the tree be taken down the next day after my birthday. I was ecstatic. One of my ideas came to fruition. I didn't let anyone see it, but inside I was having a celebration.

15

AGE: SIX

Rudy's Stuffed Kitty-cat

When I was three years old, my Mom made me a stuffed kitty pillow that was pink and soft. Pink was my favorite color. Kitty was beautiful, and I was amazed that my Mom made her for me. My Mom was so wonderful to me.

At the same time, Mom made my little sister a very similar stuffed pillow, of a blue teddy bear, which my sister loved as well.

I loved on Kitty and slept with her, carried her places, and took her on trips, for about three years. I also used to snuggle with her, when we were given permission to watch television at night. I had an assigned chair in the living room and Kitty and I used to snuggle in that chair together.

I used to suck on her ears. And after some time, her ears started to reveal little holes. These holes got bigger and bigger. Mom washed Kitty every so often to keep her clean. But she was becoming more stained as time went on. And the holes in her ears were getting obvious. The top quarter of her ears were missing.

One evening, I had been sucking on Kitty's ears, while we were all watching television. My dad suddenly got up, came straight for me and violently took Kitty from me. He told me I no longer could have Kitty. This sent me into a crying fit. I was screaming, face hot and red, and tears pouring. This upset my father more.

We had a fire burning in the fireplace at the back of the family room. Dad continued yelling at me. And I begged and pleaded for him not to take Kitty away. But he did, and said he was going to burn her up in the fireplace. The moment was brutal and heart wrenching.

He threw Kitty into the fireplace and held me back at the same time. With Daddy standing over me, I watched as Kitty quickly and nauseatingly burned. Kitty caught aflame and the fire quickly lit up her entire body. Pieces of her inside cotton fell away, lighted by fire and burned into nothing. Her body was destroyed in seconds leaving only the red burning shell of the backside fabric until it disappeared as well. I collapsed in a pile on the floor. Dad was still yelling at me, but I no longer heard his words. Mom came to my rescue at that point, picked me up, and took me to my bedroom.

My sister tore off to our room, hugging her blue bear pillow tight in her arms.

In the safety of my room, Mom promised to make me another Kitty. This didn't make me any happier. I didn't understand why Mom would say this. Within a few weeks, she had made another Cat. It was a stuffed pillow that was white with flowers that decorated its fur. It was pretty. I took it, secretly not liking it, but for Mom's sake I hugged it. I took it to my room. I never slept with her. I never loved her. I never snuggled with her. I knew she could be next in the flames of destruction, so why get attached.

16

AGE: SIX

Rain Prayer

I was so glad to be six years old. I could ride the bus with my friends. We sang songs on the way to and from school. My seat was usually in the middle of the bus. It was a happy time.

It seemed like every afternoon, on the way home, it rained. It was something that you counted on. And when it rained, it usually poured. One didn't get wet; one got drenched. And when it was my turn to get off the bus, as soon as my toes crossed the yellow line at the front, the rain would miraculously stop. I walked up the sidewalk and into my home with my mom at the door smiling and waving.

I decided to let the bus driver in on my little secret. I told her I said a rain prayer before we reached my house, and the rain would stop. Sure enough, the rain stopped. The bus was dripping wet, puddles everywhere. Yet when I reached the door to my home, I was completely dry. I waved and smiled too as the bus rolled away.

Time passed and at a school event, my mom ran into the bus driver lady and they exchanged stories about my rain prayer. My mom didn't believe it; she hadn't noticed. But after that, she said it happened over and over. She surmised that God was looking out for me.

Soothing Damages

Even in college when I rode my bike to classes, I would pray for the rain to stop until I could get into the building. I usually had design projects mounted on my bike, and if they were to get wet, I would have a mess to present in class. The rain blessing remained the same throughout college.

I'm not sure what to believe now. I still say the rain prayer sometimes, but it doesn't always work. If it has to do with faith, maybe my tank is empty.

∽

17

AGE: SIX

The Secret Contract

On her third birthday, my sister was added to the lineup for punishment. What a birthday present. My brother and I were in shock that such a little person should have to participate in this type of punishment. But there she was, standing in the lineup, waiting for her turn. She knew what to do. She'd been watching us do it for a few years, she had learned the routine. Mom knelt beside her the first few months, but Daddy made sure that ended soon enough.

My mind was racing. What could I do? There had to be something I could do to save my sister. I could lie. I could tell a big fib that I had done the deed instead of my little sister. She wouldn't correct me. She'd be glad to get out of the beating. She would be quiet for sure. It would work. Except, I couldn't take it all. I looked up at my brother standing beside me. Maybe he would help.

The next day, my brother came to me with the same thoughts. We should take credit for my little sister's wrongdoings if we could. I told him I was totally in agreement. He said it had to be a Secret Contract, that Mom and Daddy could never know. I agreed. We shook hands.

Soothing Damages
I did take some of my sister's beatings. But my brother stepped in more than he should have to accept the thrashings. He even lied for me sometimes to take my beating. I will always appreciate his protection for me and my little sister.

18

AGE: SIX

Goofy

We made yearly trips to the Magical World of Disney. As young as six years old, I would tend to get "lost" on occasion, which was not typical for me. My mom knew exactly what had happened. I had seen Goofy. So, off I had run in his direction. Mom just had to look around and find Goofy with his tall green hat and right below him she would find her daughter, me.

I loved Disney. Even my dad was happy most of the day there. He acted like a little kid. I remember the water flume ride. After waiting in line to get on the ride, Daddy would line us up on the "log," with the kids in front and him in the back. We would get soaked and he would pull out his little umbrella at the last moment and save himself and laugh and laugh. I went on the ride, not to get wet, but to hear my dad laugh. It was a great feeling.

One year we ate dinner in the Cinderella Castle. I remember it being very nice. We had to be on our best behavior that meal; we had to portray all our etiquette and manners.

Small World and the Presidents were two rides we experienced every trip. My dad thought they were educational for us. I think, too, he was partial to Small World for some reason.

Soothing Damages

My father had his good moments; they were just few and far between. I believe his probable bipolar sickness had a lot to do with his emotional imbalance. He suffered greatly.

19

AGE: SIX

S<small>TARVING</small> M<small>USICIANS</small>

And there it was, the sour note coming from my fingertips to the tune of Amazing Grace on my classic guitar. I was standing beside my brother; he was sporting his banjo. We were on center stage in front of a huge church audience. I'm sure at this point I was completely blushing red. But I kept my stature tall and my confidence strong. We moved forward through the beautiful song together and at the end we bowed and I threw in a curtsy.

We exited the stage and put our instruments away. My brother didn't say anything until it was time to go sit with our family. "Maybe he didn't notice," he said hopefully. I looked up at him. We knew Daddy had heard the error.

The first sign was when Daddy wouldn't move to let us in the row. He was on the end. We had to sit a row behind him.

He was embarrassed by our performance and by us. We sat quieter that day in church than we ever had before. Perhaps Daddy's wrath would pass. After all, we were in church and perhaps a miracle would take place. We prayed silently.

After church, people congratulated Daddy on our special music and remarked positively about it. I don't think he wanted to hear the comments because he was in a hurry for the door.

Off we zoomed in his little yellow sports car, the three of us children bunched in the back seat. There were no conversations, no words. We ended up in the parking lot at a restaurant.

Daddy said, "You and your brother stay in the car." And off went Mom, Dad and my little sister to eat dinner. My brother and I looked at each other while our stomachs gurgled. I sighed. We weren't to have any dinner. We messed up and it was my fault.

Soothing Damages

To this day, I have stage phobia. I cannot perform in front of an audience, due to this and many other experiences like it. However, I do play piano for my family on occasion. And my husband especially enjoys my music, especially the songs I wrote myself.

I was considered a master pianist when I finished taking lessons, albeit a lower level master. I was not considered especially talented, but I worked hard to get it right. I was technical.

When I was finished with high school, I wanted to be done with music. I wasn't even sure if I liked it or if it was just something I did for my father. Today I prefer writing, painting and sculpting. These interests restore and heal my soul.

20

AGE: SIX

CHRISSIE EVERT PERFECTION

I began playing tennis when I was four years old and had been playing for two years at a private liberal arts college. While at the college, I also took piano, guitar, and sculpture. These were some of my after-school and summer activities. My life was very busy.

My brother played tennis as well. He was an excellent player, or so I thought. I looked up to him. He was better than me in almost everything. He played tennis with me, and I think that is why my tennis game became much better.

We played in the sweltering heat. We would find shelter on a shady stairway. Both of us worked on the courts for the coaches, chasing tennis balls during lessons. We would both earn enough to put twenty-five cents in the soda machine, and we would buy a grape soda that we shared. It was so cold in my hand, it had droplets of cold water on the

Chapter 20

outside of the can. And it tasted like grape heaven. It was perfection.

On some days, when Dad had given my brother some money for our lunch, we would ride our bikes or walk to the Sub Pub down the way. We bought a whole steak sub and shared it. I absolutely loved that super-delicious, mouth-watering sub.

Then we went back to the courts to practice or earn coins. Our championships were coming up soon and practice was more important than ever. Our coaches were even giving us extra time to learn.

My brother qualified for a higher league. I was in my own league.

It was a hot, sunny, long day on the courts. I remember drinking lots of water whenever I had a chance at the drinking fountain. And slowly, I worked my way up the brackets. I was winning. I didn't believe I might win first place, but I was doing well. I tied one girl about my age, and we had to keep playing tie breakers. Finally, I made a point on her by returning the ball cross court, ending the game. I played one more player after that. It was dark, but we had bright lights around the courts. I was so tired I could barely run to the ball. But run I did. I knew my father was going to ask if I got first place. Not knowing exactly how, but knowing I did my best, I finished playing a great game with the last player. I had won, or thought I did.

I guess no one noticed that we had finished. The coaches were still trying to figure everything out. My mom was tired and wanted to go home, so we started off down the sidewalk toward her car. My brother said, "No, wait."

He ran back to the coaches. It took a few minutes, but he

came back with two trophies! One was for me, it was first place for my league. And he had won second place in his league. He told me that the coaches said my new nickname was Chrissie Evert.

Daddy was happy with our accomplishments that day.

Soothing Damages

My father was a well-seasoned tennis player, and he intended his children to be respectable players as well. When I think back about eating the sub with my brother or drinking the soda with him, I think the reason it tasted so good to me was because he was sharing with me, being nice to me, and caring for me. I was happy. For once, it was unconditional.

I played tennis at the private liberal arts college for eight years total while I was young.

21

AGE: SIX

Rudy's Halloween

I guess I just figured a lot of families celebrated Halloween the same way. I didn't think it was out of the ordinary in any way. It was perfectly normal for me.

The two of us got dressed in our handmade costumes. My brother was usually a ghost with a bedsheet and two holes for eyes. I was usually an American Indian. My outfit had been made for a school play. Mom helped us make our costumes. My younger sister was too young to participate this particular year.

We set out early and rushed from house to house, gathering as much candy as possible. When our bags were full, we ran back home. This worked well because our neighborhood was in the form of a big loop. So, once we had covered most of the houses, we were almost back home again anyway.

Daddy had his cardboard table out in the front yard with his chair and one candle. It was getting dark and he was waiting for us. We dumped all our candy out on his table and then went back out to get more candy from the street farther away past the loop. Daddy used the candy we had collected to give to the kids coming to our house.

I remember sweating and thinking I couldn't make it much farther by the time we reached the street where we could get our own candy. But we made it. And I remember some of the houses being very scary. We gathered enough candy to make it worthwhile and headed back home.

When we came home, Daddy had closed up shop, and the house lights were out. We came in and dumped out our candy on the kitchen table in front of Daddy. He went through each piece carefully. Anything that could be re-wrapped was thrown into the trash. No holes or tears were allowed, because it might have been tainted. Then it was time for the quality check. Anything like candy bars were lined up on one side. And sugar candies on the other. All done.

Then we would be allowed three candies, one from the candy bar side and two from the sugar candy side. If we were good children for the rest of the week, we would get repeats of this each day until the candy ran out.

Soothing Damages

I remember being told by my family that we weren't supposed to celebrate Halloween at all. That it was against our faith. I wasn't to talk about it with my friends or at church.

Somehow our candy ran out fast. I suspect my brother and father took more than their share, but I don't know. Doesn't really matter.

One year when I was about ten, I made a Wonder Woman costume and went to a neighborhood party. I was so proud of myself because I guessed how many jelly beans were in the jar.

My older brother got to wear some of my dad's old work clothes for a couple of Halloweens. He was in blue hospital scrubs those years. When my sister was old enough to participate, I remember Daddy buying masks for her.

22

AGE: SEVEN

Nurse Rudy

The water was running over my small hands. I wanted it cooler, so I waited. I put the wash rag into the cooler water and wrung it out just a bit. I grabbed my nurse bag and tiptoed to my sister's bedside.

She was small for her age. She had an attitude and was trying not to cry. But her face was red. I pulled up her nightgown and all along her back were red lash marks. I started applying the cool rag to the nape of her neck and worked my way down, trying to soothe or even will some of the pain away. These marks were too destructive for a four-year old. I reached into my little nurse bag and retrieved an antibiotic ointment. I used it sparingly, but where it was needed. I applied a few bandages. And next, I put some lotion with Vitamin E on her back to help heal her skin. Lastly, I pulled her gown back down and dabbed the cool cloth on her face a

Chapter 22

little and over her eyes. She couldn't speak a word, she just nodded. My nursing was finished for now.

It had been my sister's turn for the deed-doers round of punishment. She had left a rake in the yard after we had done our chores. My brother and I forgot to check after her like we usually did. Little kids always forgot things. We knew that, and we felt guilty.

23

AGE: SEVEN

Outlaw Leader

One of my favorite memories, even though it disrupted the entire neighborhood, was on a rainy afternoon after school. All the children on the street were out playing in the rain. We were drenched and loving every minute of it. One of the kids said that he wished the street would fill up with water so that we could have a swimming pool and we could all go swimming.

My head exploded with an idea. I knew how the rainwater worked, how it ran slightly downstream to a large drain down the road. If I could just keep the water from going down the drain, I could fill up the street with water. We were on the low side of the street, so it shouldn't take long to fill it up. I gathered a band of outlaws and we went on an adventure. We were going to build a dam.

We had the greatest of times building that dam. We used

the free tar rocks from the road, mixed with soil and sand. We added little twigs to give it some strength. Then bigger sticks and more road mix, soil and sand. I had friends bringing buckets of the stuff from up the way. And my best friend and I were pounding the mud-mix into a dam formation, all the way around the three sides of the drain. We had a little trouble at the end because the water wanted to rush through, but we remained formidable. The dam was quite large by the end. The fourth side was already walled in by the built-in curbing. The miracle was that it held fiercely. We had succeeded.

The street slowly filled. I put two of my outlaws on dam duty to call me if the water fortress burst open. Everyone else played in the street, which had filled with water. It was a glorious and beautiful day.

I think we had a blissful, happy hour or so before the fathers came home to find their houses partially flooded.

At our house, only the front yard and the front entry area was flooded. Mom had that cleaned up quickly after the water receded.

Inevitably, one of the dads came looking for me. I was the leader of the outlaws. All the children were sent home and the dam was demolished forevermore. My pride and passion washed down that big square drain with the last of the rainwater.

I had time to clean up and wait for my Dad to come home. He would give me my punishment. And home he came. Mom told him what had happened, and he shrugged his shoulders. That was strange. He acted as if nothing had happened. My punishment didn't transpire. I could not believe it.

Soothing Damages

My father didn't punish me. I still don't understand why. I knew I was to never do it again. But to not be punished was a reward. My mom sent me to my room, which was probably wise.

I think my father liked a little rebellion in me. Who knows? He may have liked the fact that his daughter had the wit and intelligence to mastermind the neighborhood dam. It was interesting. It wasn't my usual mode of operation, the obedient, good girl routine. If I had learned from this, I would have been more of a rebel. But I did not. I liked being the well-behaved girl; I believed that in the long run it would pay off.

24

AGE: SEVEN

Toys for Boys

Our two aunts, Daddy's sisters, were taking us to the toy store. We were all excited. First, we ate breakfast. My brother ate sugared flakes cereal, and my sister and I ate regular flakes cereal. Boys ate what they wanted, and girls did not. Then we dressed in our everyday clothes, brushed our teeth and ran to the car. It was going to be a great day. We were going shopping and all we could talk about was the toy store and all the toys we wanted. We would pick one toy. Thinking about the many various toy possibilities was so much fun. We arrived at the store and our aunts set down a few guide rules. Our older aunt was going to take our brother into the store. Our younger aunt was going to take us girls into the store. Sounded good to me. Boys and girls liked different things.

My older aunt and brother disappeared into the back of

the store. The girly toys were on the other side of the store anyway, so off we went on our adventure. We found bright, shiny, new dolls of all kinds with clothes and accessories of all kinds. We were delighted with anticipation, until my older aunt showed up in our aisle and took our other aunt aside for a few minutes before leaving. Our aunt looked at us for a while; I knew something was up. Then she took us by the hands and said she wanted to show us a variety of toys that we could pick from. A little confused we left all the dolls and other toys behind and followed her to the front of the store near the register. There was a round, turning wire rack there. It was about as tall as we were. And there were little toys hanging on it like little tree ornaments. I looked at the top of the rack and it said, "10 cent toys."

2ND - 3RD GRADE

My breath left my body. My face got warm. I couldn't believe what was happening. While my sister and I were standing there confounded, a man with a box that was taller than me, dragged it up to the front register.

Following the man, was my older aunt and my brother. Of course, I thought, my brother gets the big toy and we get the little toys. It all made sense.

Why I didn't see it earlier was my own foolishness. My aunt told me to pick my toy out, and I said I didn't want one. And she said I had to. My little sister didn't want one either. So, I picked two naked dolls about four inches tall with no hair, no painted faces, and they were a transparent beige, very thin plastic.

The two dolls cost twenty cents.

And now my aunts could tell our parents that they bought us toys. But I didn't say anything. What good would that do? A girl didn't have a voice. I knew that. And my sister was learning that as well. We felt betrayed and unimportant.

The ride home was traumatic. My sister and I were gloomy. My brother was elevated. We tried to be nice and asked him about his toy. He was so excited about it. He said it was an electric football field with little football players that moved across the field all by themselves. To make matters worse, the box was so big it was sticking out the back end of the car. It just made the whole experience that much more of a contrast.

When we got home, we unboxed my brother's gift and set it up, so he could play with it. He was so proud. I would be too. He plugged it in and turned it on. It made a lot of noise and the players moved across the field. Some of them made loops in the field, some ran straight, and some ran the wrong way – much like real football. My sister and I tired of our brother's new prized possession quickly and retired to our rooms while he stayed out in the living room with my two aunts laughing and having a good time. They would show my dad the new toy.

My sister and I kept the little dolls. We dressed them and put little bonnets on them. We put them into our pink and white hand-crocheted purses that hung down like little cribs in the breeze. We carried them to church on occasion. But mostly they stayed nestled in their beds.

25

AGE: SEVEN

Beach Summer

My family used to love spending time at the beach. The year I was seven years old they bought a condo in one of the buildings along the shore in Brevard County, Florida. This beach turned into my haven. For the summers my family would go their separate ways. Mom, my sister and I went to the beach condo and my dad and brother stayed at home in the city. I think my Mom and Dad needed a break from each other sometimes, and it was a relief for me to get away from Daddy. I used to feel sorry for my brother having to stay, but that's the way my parents decided to do things.

We had a schedule we adhered to at the beach: sun in the morning, lunch and math/English activities at noon when the sun was high, and sun in the evening until we wanted to go inside. We worked on the wisemen craft that is known in our family. There are three wisemen in each set;

each standing about sixteen inches tall. The bases are made from styrofoam, thick wire, cloth and glue. Then we cover them in red, purple, and blue velvet robes and capes, with faux gem crowns and detailed trims and lace usually golden or silver. We also worked on dollhouse furniture kits, building and painting pieces. We loved to color in our coloring books. Food was always fun and yummy; Mom made homemade taco salads, tacos, vegetarian corn dogs, cheddar tuna pockets, subs, pizzas and more.

Our days in the sun were mostly spent in the pool swimming laps or just playing and splashing around. We loved the water. Our skin would get golden brown. Out on the beach we took walks, gathered shells, built sandcastles, played in the surf, body surfed, and jumped waves.

There was also a recreation room attached to the condo building. It had a pool table, ping-pong table, sauna, jacuzzi, and workout room. We mostly used the ping-pong table. But there was plenty to keep us busy. It was a great getaway each year.

∼

26

AGE: EIGHT

College Mom

I snuck out of my room after everyone was supposed to be asleep in the house. There was a light on in the family room. Keeping my footsteps soft, I headed for the light to see what was going on. And there I found Mom. She was asleep, sitting with her face in her book and artwork spread out in front of her. She must have been exhausted. I woke her gently and sent her off to bed. I found her like that often enough.

I knew it was hard for her to work for Dad, keep house, take care of us children and Daddy, and go to college. There was not enough time for all of it, but she endured.

On my mom's class days, if I was not in school, she would bring me with her. I had to promise not to say a word and to be still. So, I did. I sat in a chair next to her workstation. She would paint at an easel and listen to the professor lecture. I used to watch her paint and wish I could do the same. It was fascinating what Mom could do. She created some beautiful artwork.

Mom attended classes for a total of two and a half years in art college. But my dad was relentless in the amount of work he expected from her. So, inevitably, Mom dropped out of college to care for us and Daddy. I may have had a hand in that as well. I remember telling my mom that we didn't see much of her and we missed her.

Soothing Damages

Ironically, after my father passed away in my thirties, Mom blossomed in art. She took it further than she ever thought she would. I consider her to be a master artist today. She has taken many classes from art galleries and such. And we all – Mom, my aunt, and I – painted together in her art studio for many years. We still get together and paint. It's such a fulfillment for my heart and soul.

27

AGE: EIGHT

Calico Drive-Over

I was getting dressed and helping dress my little sister. Daddy was going to come home from work and pick us up. We were headed to a Friday night gathering at the church. My mother liked it when my sister and I dressed alike. We wore our red and white gingham dresses with white lace trim. We also had little matching purses with baby dolls hidden inside. We finished it all off with brushing our teeth, washing our faces and brushing our hair. My sister liked her hair in ponytails.

Mom, my brother, my sister and I stood in the driveway just outside the door waiting for my Dad to arrive in his two-door sports car. We played with our cats, Calico and Blackie, while we waited. Calico was pregnant. She was slow and tired. She would have her babies soon. Calico was my favorite. A three-colored cat was special; she was a cool cat.

We heard Daddy's car coming, and sure enough there he was. He drove into the driveway and slowed down as Calico plopped herself right down on the driveway in front of his car. Daddy roared the engine and honked the horn. Calico just lay there. My Dad then proceeded to drive forward slowly and drove over Calico's tummy area. She got up and hobbled over to the neighbor's house and hid. We could not find her and had to go to church, so we left her hurt and alone.

All I could think about was Calico the whole evening until we got back home. When we did get home that night, Mom and the three of us children searched for Calico and finally found her in the neighbor's side yard.

We put her into a box with some rags. She wasn't bleeding but she was flattened in her tummy area. Mom said she didn't know if Calico or the babies would survive. We left them in the garage for the night. And we all went to bed. There was nothing more that we could do.

The next morning Calico had birthed five long slender kittens. Calico passed away during the night. We fed the kittens milk in baby-doll bottles. But the kittens only survived for three days.

Soothing Damages

I think my father was thinking that Calico would move if he drove forward slowly, but I don't know. I don't remember him honking. I do not think though that he should have taken the risk to keep moving forward. I remember thinking that my father would stop before he ran her over but he didn't. And his attitude on the matter was disgusting as he was inclined not to care at all about Calico. Mom and us kids buried Calico and the kittens. My father wanted nothing to do with it.

I was traumatized by the event. I remember Mom and Dad telling us not to talk about it at church that night, and that's all I could think about. I don't think I spoke or interacted with anyone too much that evening until we returned home again.

28

AGE: NINE

First Diet

Mom sat me down at the round kitchen table. My finger followed the design of the sunflower on the tablecloth in front of me. I knew something was wrong. She wanted my attention, so I tucked my hands down and away, and looked at Mom.

I had told her previously that the kids at school were making fun of me because they thought I was fat. They were calling me names like Fat Cat, Fatty and Fat Girl. I was in a new school that year too, so it made it doubly difficult for me. And I liked one of the boys, but I worried that he thought I was fat too.

In my mom's conversation, she made it clear that she wanted me to be happy with myself. But I did feel that she and Dad wanted me to lose some weight. It wasn't good for a member of his family to be overweight. I remember the doctor told me I was a little overweight, but that I would probably grow out of it.

So, I went on a diet of no bread or extra carbs, one dessert a week only, and no sodas. I remember on Sunday mornings the smell of fresh donuts on the table that I couldn't have. Or the smell of fresh homemade chocolate chip pecan cookies coming out of the oven. It was hard watching my family eat food I could not have, but I stuck to it. It took about a year for the weight to come off and I moved on.

4TH GRADE

Soothing Damages

I struggled with weight gain and diets most of my life. Sometimes I would be strong and would look great and other times I gained it all back. I have always wondered if my weight had something to do with wanting to blend in and be an accepted part of the family or wanting to not be seen. This was and still is one of my coping devices. If no one sees me, then I won't get into trouble.

29

AGE: TEN

SNOW WHITE

"Just whistle while you work," I sang barely audibly, sweeping the floor in the kitchen. I had just finished cleaning the dishes, pots and pans, and countertops. Soon my chores would end and I could work on my homework in the sanctuary of my room. The song kept me happy when doing routine chores and gave me a mental escape. I always did my chores correctly, doing them with strength, quality and timeliness. Mom and Dad knew that when they gave a chore to me, they would not have to check after me when I was finished. They knew it would be done to his standards. "Just hum a merry tune," I finished up and moved on to my next phase of the evening, which was homework.

Homework had a different musical need. I played one of my cassette tapes on my mini stereo with "Bach" written on it. I had several Bach tapes. All of them helped me study. I put the music on low, so as not to bother Dad, and studied like a maniac. I was an A-level student most of the time.

On work days, like Sundays, we did chores all day long and into the late evening. I sang silently on those days, so as not to be heard. But I enjoyed working in nature. It was the inside work that was more stressful for me.

Soothing Damages
My character traits of strength, quality, and timeliness — and of good grades in school — these qualities came out of fear. My fear was of my father being angry and hurting me mentally or physically. I've always wondered if these characteristics are really mine, or do they stem from the fear. Did those fears shape me into a more successful adult? Are we merely a kind of robot, born and then programmed by fear?

30

AGE: TWELVE

W̲ha̲t̲ ̲i̲s̲ ̲L̲ove̲

We still lived in our home in Florida when I decided I needed to tell someone about my relationship with Regnad. Our relationship had progressed, and he had been trying to have intercourse with me the last few times we had played our games together.

I was scared. I did not want it to happen. I didn't know what it was, but I knew I didn't like it. I had an impression that it was not right. But I trusted him and loved him, so I wasn't sure about any of it.

I had tried to convince Reg that we should not try to do this, but he became upset with me for suggesting that we stop playing games. He said the game was important to him and how dare I take that game away from him. We were friends, and I owed him. I had promised to play the game with him. And I had promised to keep it secret. And if I was his friend, how come I wanted the game to stop.

Maybe Mom would help me. Maybe she would make Reg stop playing this game with me. I told Mom I needed to speak with her. She made some time, and we sat at the little round kitchen table by the window. The curtains had sunflower designs on them, and the matching tablecloth did also.

I told her about the game and that it was supposed to be a secret. She asked me a few questions about the game. She was agitated; I knew the conversation wasn't going well. She didn't like what she was hearing. I had done something wrong for sure.

She asked me if I knew what sex was. And I gave her a firm negative answer. But her questions made me think that what I was explaining was sex after all. She didn't say another word. She didn't explain anything. She just picked up the phone behind her and called Daddy.

Mom told Daddy that he was to come home immediately. But Daddy said he had work and would be home after work was finished. Mom and I waited, not saying much at all. She swept and cleaned the kitchen, eyeing me, but never saying anything. I felt terrible. My stomach felt so sick.

And then Daddy came home. "Now what's this all about?"

Never using the word "sex", my mother repeated my story to Dad. My mother was furious. But Daddy was indifferent.

"We can find out if this is true or not right now." He lifted the phone and called Reg at his home. When he came to the phone, Daddy asked him about me. And Reg denied everything.

And that was that. Daddy hung up the phone, angrier than ever. "And you believe her? She's lying. She's just trying to get attention."

Things with Reg were never the same after that. He treated me as if I were invisible to him. No more smiles, hugs, or kind words.

Soothing Damages

I am just a female. Females have no authority. We have no voice. At times I felt as though I had no soul. Why is being a female so much less than everything else? Maybe because we are the weaker sex and some men tend to take advantage of it. I'm sorry. How am I supposed to respect that point of view? Just because you are stronger physically, you will beat me into submission?

That's what I was taught. That's what I've had to unlearn. I don't think most men understand because they haven't been in the situation. I think my father lacked the empathy to understand his actions when he said I was lying.

I tended to search out men who beat up women. Not intentionally, but because it was something I was used to. Even though I didn't like being beaten, it was something I was comfortable with. It was a psychological pattern I followed, one I had to banish so I could start over.

31

AGE: TWELVE TO EIGHTEEN

THE MOUNTAIN HOUSE

I was what seemed like two stories up the ladder, at the top, with a stain can in one hand and a paintbrush in the other. Daddy got the great idea of leaning the ladder a bit, so I could reach farther to the left and right. I was not afraid of heights, until after this day. I was able to reach farther. But after leaning the ladder too far, the inevitable happened. I fell with my stain can and all. Luckily nothing was broken. And up the ladder I went again. It was a learning curve for all of us, I suppose.

This was our mountain house in North Carolina. We had moved here when I was twelve. The three of us children stained the room we shared on the first level. My brother stained the top logs. I stained the middle logs and my sister painted the bottom logs. We accomplished our mission quite well.

The balconies, my brother and I stained. There was the larger balcony on the main floor and the two smaller balconies on the top floor. We brushed the stain on thicker to the floor boards than we did to the building logs; they soaked it up more.

The basement balcony on the back of the house had a concrete pad at ground level; we cleaned this with Clorox and soap to strip the algae, mold and dirt. I enjoyed this cleaning part of the job because we used water and cleaning supplies. In contrast, the stain had a slight burning sensation to the skin. So, the water felt good and refreshing for a change.

Cleaning windows on the outside was always fun too. My sister started volunteering for the higher windows since she was small and light. We held the ladder firmly for her.

Cleaning out the garage and the storage shed was part of the process as well. We would go through everything, taking it out, prioritizing items and figuring out what needed to stay and what needed to go. We cleaned out the two spaces and then, in an organized fashion, we placed things back into storage. My favorite part was organizing the tools and hanging them up on the pegboard or putting them in the large toolbox in the toolshed. We tried very hard to pass inspection. Very rarely did Daddy complain when we cleaned, stained and reorganized for him.

I think the most fun in the whole procedure was restocking and organizing the pantry room, cellar room and large box freezer. I loved organizing items of any kind. I would place the newer items in the back and pull the older products closer to the front, always placing the front of the object face forward. The pantry was fun because it was full of color and different foodstuffs. We had shelves on both sides of the room, and it was long. Cases were stacked at the bottom, on the floor. The five-gallon containers of dried milk, rice, dried beans, and salt were also stored on the floor in the pantry. Mostly cans and preserve jars were stacked on the shelves containing a variety of vegetables, beans, vegetarian proteins and more from our garden and the store. We made all sorts of preserves including sauerkraut, pickles, and apple butter.

Lastly, we raked the parking area around the house and the gravel road down to a water well that was a quarter of a mile down the road. The goal was to level out the gravel so there were no tire trenches in view. I enjoyed this work too. It was hard, but it was time I could just be by myself and think.

Soothing Damages

I remember being taught that we moved to the wilderness to get away from the bigger cities. And that if the end of time came, we would be prepared to live through it. I knew about seven families from our church lived all over our mountain.

We helped and supported one another.

I'm not sure if the storage of so much food was a religious idea, or if my father just thought we may go hungry like he did when he was a child.

The whole idea taught me to be prepared. I'm a squirrel by design. Hiding my acorns away out of sight. I have a pantry now too that people tease me about. But it is not even a quarter of the size of my family's old pantry.

32

AGE: TWELVE TO EIGHTEEN

Beans and Rice

After a long day at school and then long hours working at Dad's office, he would drive us home. As soon as we would arrive at home, Mom started cooking dinner and we would ask, "What kind of beans are we having tonight?" Beans and rice, that was dinner. Every Monday through Friday our meals never changed. There were white beans, butter beans, large lima beans, red beans, kidney beans, pink beans, black beans, black-eyed peas, lentils, and more. We tried it all. Sometimes Mom stewed the beans with tomatoes, onions, and celery. Other times it was just the beans. We did on occasion, when Mom sautéed chopped onions, dump our salads onto our rice and beans and mix it all up with the onions. Sometimes Mom would even add cooked tomatoes. This was called Jacob's Pottage. And it gave the meal a nice twist. Luckily, we all liked beans and rice for the most part. It was just a little difficult to eat them every day.

On Thursday evenings, Daddy took us out to eat on the way home, so Mom wouldn't have to cook. We always ate at the country inn restaurant. They had a wonderful variety of hot vegetables there. And by this time, we had started to eat meat, so chicken or chopped steak was usually the entrée. Daddy ordered for each of us, he even ordered for Mom, it was usually the special or the best value on the menu. The waitresses knew to bring us lemon juice packets and sugar packets, so we could make our own lemonade. Daddy must have made a good living in the medical field, but he didn't want to pay for anything he didn't have to.

On Saturday nights, we had a tradition of warming up frozen pizzas and adding our own toppings to them. We added extra cheese, vegetarian sausage, onions, peppers, etc. And Sunday nights, we made sub rolls. Sometimes we had ice cream on Saturday or Sunday evenings.

Soothing Damages

I don't think we ever complained about beans and rice. It was our staple meal. I think it saved my family money for several years and put food on the table that was nourishing.

Feeding three children was a tall order I am sure. I think my dad put his money toward the house mortgage, family cars, and his office rent mainly.

I know he sent money to his two sisters who lived together. I think he felt obligated to them because they

Chapter 32

raised him. His mother didn't want much to do with him. He was born last; he was much younger than his older siblings.

33

AGE: TWELVE TO SIXTEEN

Driving Lessons

At age twelve, my dad taught me to use the steering wheel while he drove the jeep. Up and down the mountain gravel roads I would practice. I landed us in the ditch a few times, but at least I never drove off the cliff. It was a very narrow road up and down the mountainside. He also let me get a feel of changing the gears for him occasionally.

At age fourteen, Daddy had me start driving the jeep. It was a grey Toyota Land Cruiser with a long stick shift. Daddy said that if I learned how to drive the "Goat," as we called her, I could drive anything. On the way home, when we hit private property, Dad had me get behind the wheel. I remember having a little trouble with the clutch, but since I had learned to ride a motorcycle here in the mountains, the gear shifting made sense to me. I just had to make the adjustments of hand versus foot.

At age sixteen, I took the driver's writing class at the public high school and tied for first place. I received one hundred percent in the class, along with another girl. We were friends and were both overjoyed to have first pick on when we got to do the driving part of the class. We picked the first weekend at the school. After passing with flying colors, we were able to receive our driver learner's permits.

Driving my family from place to place with Dad in the passenger seat was very stressful. One wrong move and he exploded. Every move had to be smooth, efficient and perfect.

When going to the grocery store one day, I was slowing into the left lane to take a left turn up ahead. A semi-truck was coming toward us from the opposite direction. My dad told me to, "Go, go, go!" I slowed at the end of the left turning lane and was terrified, I didn't want to go but Dad had told me to, so I hit the gas pedal and turned the jeep toward the entryway to the grocery store. Then Dad was shouting, asking, "Why did you go? Are you an idiot?"

I am positive that the semi-truck had to hit his brakes very hard not to hit us. My Dad was livid and yelling at me. I think my family was in shock. I was in shock. All I could say was, "I shouldn't have gone."

All I could think was that I could have killed us all. They left me in the car to go grocery shopping. It was fine with me. I had time to try to absorb what had happened and try to figure out how to handle Dad's rantings and ravings while navigating oncoming eighteen-wheelers.

`Soothing Damages`

I learned quite quickly to listen to my own judgment and not let my father have the last word when driving. Mere seconds defined life and death. Decisions had to be made swiftly. My driving enraged him several times after that, but at least we were safe. That's what mattered to me. It had taken sixteen years but I was learning to stand up to him when it mattered most.

34

AGE: TWELVE TO FOURTEEN

Family Ice Cream

I remember riding in the Land Cruiser with my dad through the mountain roads. I never asked where we were headed. If he didn't tell me where we were going, I was not meant to know. I usually daydreamed; it helped me keep my mouth shut and my body still. He slowed down "The Goat" and down-shifted, heading down a short hill and into a parking lot to an industrial-looking building.

In we went, and a man met us at the door, shaking Daddy's hand. He invited us inside and took us to a room-size freezer; it was so cold in there. Daddy asked about the chocolate chip, the chocolate, and the mint chocolate chip ice cream and where they were located. The three-gallon brown containers were cylindrical in shape and full of ice cream. I helped carry one of the containers to the Toyota.

Daddy asked for any more milk crates, and the man gave

Daddy a few. He loved to use the milk crates at home for organizing items.

Daddy said we needed to race home now, before the ice cream could melt. So, we did. It took us thirty minutes instead of the usual forty. Into our large box freezer in the basement went the three cylinders of ice cream.

We had an ice cream party that night after dinner. For dinner we had homemade subs with sub rolls, deli meats and cheeses, lettuce, tomato, onion, peppers, Italian spices, oil and vinegar, and mustard and mayonnaise. We would toast the meats and cheese on the rolls and then dress them how each person liked them best. This was one of our family traditions. We all loved it.

Everyone was happy about the arrival of the ice cream, including Daddy. And we all had our favorite flavors too. The chocolate chip was for Dad and Mom; the mint was for my brother and the chocolate was for my sister and me. We sat and watched a movie together on the television.

On a regular weekend, when we had chores on Sundays, my brother, sister and I would sneak ice cream between chores from the basement freezer. My brother would sneak spoons from the kitchen upstairs and bring them down to us. And we would have a mini-party. I could usually get away with it easily because I did laundry a lot, and the washer and dryer were in the same room as the large freezer unit.

Chapter 34

Soothing Damages

The ice cream cylinders became a family tradition. Sometimes the flavors would change, but these basic flavors were our standards. We would have ice cream about once a week as a family. It was nice to have good times, happy times. Ice cream reminds me of those times.

35

AGE: TWELVE TO FOURTEEN

BURNING TIME

My dad believed that if we were busy, we wouldn't get into any trouble. Sunday was chore day. One of the chores we had to do was to clean out dead wood and vines from our woods. This was a tough job and it seemed never ending. It was an endless chore but I loved working outside. I never liked being chosen to work inside. Outside there was fresh air and sunlight and of course, less chance of catching Daddy's wrath. And the forest was beautiful and wild. I would dress for battle and wear my overalls, flannel shirt, hat, boots and leather gloves. It was going to be an encounter with Mother Nature. And she would win; she always did. We tried to tame her but she would grow wild again. I loved it.

We started in the morning after breakfast. We ate well on mornings like these; we devoured eggs, vegetarian sausage, and toast or grits along with some juice. About mid-morning, Mom would bring out extra-strong lemonade, my favorite part of the day.

We each had an axe assigned to us. My brother had the big axe; I had the medium axe and my sister was supposed to haul everything to help build a fire. We used the axes, saws and clippers to cut everything; we also used shovels to dig up the vine roots. Sometimes we raked up piles of dead brush.

I got into trouble a few times when I did this as there was a yellow jacket hive next to the vine root. Out of the nest flew stinging wasps. We counted my stings one time and they numbered more than three hundred. My dad gave me medicine for swelling and I had the rest of the day off after that. Other times we ran into snakes, fire ants, skunks, rabbits, deer, wolves, foxes, armadillos, and other creatures. The meetings with snakes always ended up badly on their part, luckily. If it was a friendly snake, we usually let them go.

We would drag all the dead wood and vines to a pile on the gravel road. The pile of wood grew into a massive heap. Sometimes we had to get the Toyota to pull out larger pieces. We would use the chain or rope depending on the challenge. On the bigger logs, my brother had to cut them up with a chainsaw. I cut down branches with an axe and carried those up the hillside.

Around noon my dad would light the debris pile with gasoline and matches; a roaring fire would reduce everything into charcoal dust by the late evening, sometimes into the early night. We would then water everything down for the night. All that was left was a charcoal mark on the gravel. These were long, hard days. I would be dirty from head to toe, and I would be exhausted. Showering was such a relief.

Soothing Damages

I have fond memories of working in the forest. I imagined that I was cleaning one of God's gardens. I loved working with nature and in nature. It felt right, and it felt like I was home.

Getting stung by wasps was just part of life. You experience chaos, and then you move on. Nature made sense to me.

Burning the dead wood was warming and marked a passing of old dead things. That too had a soothing sense about it. It was nice to let things go.

36

AGE: TWELVE

Kitty-cats on the Roof

Cally (short for Calico) had a litter of six kittens at the mountain home. Cally was a descendant of the ill-fated Calico that we had in Florida. We had just adopted Frisky (our mutt puppy). He was very little at the time, and we would find all of them snuggled in the box together like one family. Cally took care of Frisky like she was one of her newborn kittens.

During the day, the animals would stay in the garage huddled together because it was a cold time of year. At night, Mom, my sister and I would sneak the animals upstairs into my sister's room and my room for the nights. Luckily, the animals were quiet. They were young and not very loud. A little time passed, and the kittens were getting big enough to walk and run a tad.

On Sabbath, we went to church. When we came back

home, my dad was in one of his moods. He was unhappy with us for one reason or another. The day had warmed up a little and Cally had all the babies out for a walk in the parking area in front of the house. Dad parked the jeep, got out and grabbed a baby kitten. He threw it up on the roof of the house. We were all perplexed. "Dad what are you doing?"

"Just watch," He laughed. He picked up two more baby kittens and threw them up on the roof too. Cally was trying to figure out a way up to the roof. She looked anxious, which describes how I felt. She finally decided to jump onto the Land Cruiser and then onto the roof. It took her a few tries, but she was desperate, and she succeeded. She immediately grabbed one kitten in her mouth and jumped straight down to the ground, dropping it and jumping back onto the jeep and then the roof for the next kitten.

Daddy was laughing and thought it was a game. Frisky came over and decided to get under Daddy's feet. Daddy swung back his leg and kicked Frisky into the air. She made a terrible sound and went flying. Meanwhile, we begged him to stop what he was doing.

My sister went to rescue Frisky. My brother and I started picking up the kittens and running away from Daddy. When he had nothing more to do, he went inside, slammed the door and locked us outside in our dress clothes with the animals. So, we waited.

Soothing Damages

It was just more trauma for me as a child. I love animals and I am gentle with them. After seeing what my father did to these helpless creatures, I never wanted to see that cruelty repeated to any animal. The rest of us showed our love for animals when we worked against my father. Our father was not one to be crossed easily. We chose to cross him and to accept the punishment he doled out when we acted to save the animals. It was the right decision.

I think that sometimes the right decision in life is not the easy decision. I know I've run into this a lot in my lifetime. It can be punishing to make the right decision for ourselves and for those around us.

37

AGE: TWELVE

The Motorcycle

One day a few people drove up with a small trailer; and on the trailer was a Honda 200cc motorcycle. My brother already had a motorbike. My father called me out of the house. I had been working with my mother. I came outside and Dad asked me if I had seen a bike like this before. It was a Honda 200cc highway/off-road model. It was silver and black; I thought it was nice looking. It had a double seat. Then Dad told one of the men to go ahead and teach me how to ride the motorbike.

I thought I was supposed to ride a motorcycle. My mind couldn't wrap itself around the information, much less listen to the trainer. I watched more than I listened. And after donning a jacket, a silver helmet, gloves and my boots, I straddled the bike. I had to stand tippy-toe, and the bike was heavy. But I managed. I was determined to make this work. We practiced getting on and off the bike, picking up the bike from the ground into a standing position and starting it with the choke or without.

My mom came out of the house a few times and made sure Dad knew that she did not like the situation. Then she'd turn and go back inside. Dad sat in his lawn chair and quietly watched the process.

Finally, I was taught by example how to drive down the gravel road. I knew I could handle this. Down the road I went, slowly in first gear the whole way there and back. Awesome, I thought. Well, now they wanted me to hit second gear. I rode down the road again and hit second gear there and back. Then it was third gear that they wanted. That meant faster gear changing and speed. I left a trail of dust and gravel in my tracks. I was free. This was the coolest thing ever. It was still difficult to remember everything, but I was positive that I would become a professional. I just needed a little more experience.

There was a second helmet; it was orange. It was for my sister. I was to take her with me on trips. We often took many motorcycle rides through the woods, on and off trails. We found some of the most beautiful places in the mountains like waterfalls, grassy meadows and rocky caves. We had a load of fun with that bike.

Some weekends, from Friday evening until Sunday evening, my sister and I would just leave home and go camping in the woods. It was our way of getting away from Dad and all the drama. We would take the bike to somewhere new or to our usual place up at the top of the ridge.

We had a two-man tent, food and water, and sleeping bags. We would bike or hike during the days or just sit and talk.

Mom would usually go on a hike to check on us. Sometimes she'd bring us a treat. All the animals would follow her. Sometimes she would sit and join us. It was peaceful.

38

AGE: TWELVE

Pansy Face Garden

My all-time favorite flower was a ruffled purple-and-white petalled flower with a black smiley-face painted on it. No matter what I said to her, she smiled back at me. She was a friendly little thing. She was beautiful, bright, happy, and made great company. I was sitting on the rock steps that led down from our log cabin home down into the woods below. My mom and I had worked on this garden together. Moving large rocks for steps, and smaller rocks for borders. We planted lilies, Indian paintbrushes, buttercups, asters, bellflowers, primroses, pansies and more. The pansies cross pollinated and some remarkably beautiful flowers were created in the process.

I came here often by myself in the evenings if we came home before sundown and I didn't have chores. I would sit in the garden and softly sing songs from classic musicals or I would just talk quietly. I knew I would get a smile out of at least one flower.

At the bottom of the rock stairs on the hillside was a garden that we built with railroad ties. We had planted green beans, tomatoes, strawberries, cucumbers, carrots and potatoes. Some things we found in the wild: raspberries, blackberries and buckberries. We also shared gardens with our five neighbors, who were all within six miles from our home. They had apples, grapes, and all sorts of vegetables. That added a variety to what we put into our basement pantry and basement root cellar. We would travel to each other's houses and help with harvesting, cleaning, cooking, preserving, canning, and more. We made jams, juices, applesauces, tomato breads, and preserved all vegetables. Mom made her famous apple butter sauce. Its presence permeated the entire mountain. All the neighbors could smell that aroma and they would come with cups and jars for a sample or even a jar of it. We also made pickles and sauerkraut; these were some foul-smelling processes.

My father was paid for some of his medical services with a bag of tomatoes, or a bag of cucumbers, or a bag of apples, or a puppy dog. This is the way things were done in the Appalachian Mountains. It was how we survived.

Soothing Damages

My mom's favorite flower was the pansy. She's the one who taught me about their little smiles.

Harvesting and preserving food seemed to be fun for me. It was interesting to learn different techniques.

Buckberries grew on the mountain; they were new to us. They were like blueberries, and very flavorful. Mom's buckberry jam was also popular. That was another tasty item that Mom made that the neighbors sought after. We also gave these buckberry jars away as gifts throughout the year or for Christmas.

39

AGE: TWELVE

Love Burns

He had done it again. My big brother had run away. Daddy was so mad, so angry. He scared me so much, I was terrified. He ordered me to follow him down the stairs. We were going to my brother's room; I knew it.

But we didn't go to his room first. We went to the furnace room and I helped Daddy get some coals and we put them into the fireplace in the basement. Daddy just cursed and said bad things until he went silent. I mechanically did what I thought Daddy wanted. We were building a decent fire. He yelled at me a few times, but he seemed to be in his own world, stewing over my brother.

At some point, Daddy hastened for my brother's room. I followed reluctantly. Daddy started throwing my brother's belongings to me. Once my arms were full of precious keepsakes like teddy bears, toys, clothing, bedsheets, pillows, papers, and books, we headed for the fireplace. There were things that I had given to my brother. There were things that other family members had given him.

In a whisper I begged Daddy not to continue, that my brother would be back. He would need these things for school. I think I made him angrier. He just grabbed one item at a time from my arms and threw it in the fire, waiting for it to come aflame and then throw in the next item. I wept through the whole process. I did what I was told, even though I didn't want to.

My brother's room grew bare as we made each trip. We burned possessions for an eternity that evening. I wondered if my tears would run out.

We accomplished Daddy's objective. This is how Daddy loved us. When love goes wrong, it is not forgiven. It is burnt into flames.

And then there were a small collection of rocks, a small collection of belt buckles, and some small iron-cast toy cars. In the closet were empty wire hangers. These last items went into a trash bag and into the outdoor trash can. The mattress was bare. No one lived in that room. Not anymore. My heart sank.

Soothing Damages

As I grew older, I realized my father's behavior was not normal. His behavior was erratic and didn't make sense to me. He accused us of things we didn't do and then punished us for those things. His actions were mean and cruel. I began to understand that my father had his own issues to deal with from his own experiences. We were mistreated and punished, but maybe it was for something he had done instead of something we had done. Despite everything, we had our mother. She comforted us and loved us.

Maybe when my father was a kid, he had his belongings burned or was mistreated similarly. Or maybe my father had done something wrong and he was punishing my brother for his own mistake. All we know now are the scars.

∼

40

AGE: THIRTEEN TO TWENTY THREE

My Plan

When I was a teenager, I realized that I was trapped. I had to follow my family's teachings and follow their traditions if I lived under their roof. If I were to leave my family, I would end up on the street. I had nowhere to go. My plan was simple. Follow the rules until I had a degree of my own and I could get a job, or alternatively until I got married. I could get married after I graduated with a degree from college. Both choices would land about the same time in my life.

I had less and less interest in our religion, and more and more interest in spirituality. I found the origins of religion fascinating. And the study of other religions and philosophies was mind-blowing. I was studying books that were not on our reading list. I wanted to be ready for the world when I flung myself out into it. I knew my church was only a small part of what the world had to offer. And I learned that asking questions and searching was a very dangerous road to follow in the eyes of my family and the church I attended.

My dad had a long discussion with me about my career in life. He gave me three education choices that he would help finance: a doctor, a lawyer, or an architect, in that order. At the end of the conversation I chose to be an architect because I was artistically talented. And I knew I could not make it through school alone. He didn't necessarily like it, but he could live with my decision. He told Mom that he had wanted me to follow him into his profession and share his practice with him.

To move my plan along, I would need to head to a public college somewhere along the way – if I could convince my family to allow this. Daddy wanted me to graduate from the same religious institution that he did. If I chose something outside the norm, maybe our church schools wouldn't have the educational support needed for such a degree. But, of course it did, or we thought so. For a year I went to a church boarding college in the North. I was one of the top students, and one of the professors took pity on me. He advised me that the school was not accredited in this degree. He advised me to leave the church college and go to a public university so that I could receive a real education. Part of my plan had worked out. I was headed to a public university.

So, onward I aspired. Step by step, I was fulfilling my plan. I was in cultural shock my first year or two of college. The girls wore makeup, mini-skirts and jewelry. They painted their nails colors. The teachers cursed in class. The boys flirted. I became a real introvert until my first friend came along in my second year. She and I were assigned a design project together and together we received the best grade in the class. She latched on to me after that. And I became friends with her group of companions. We were all quirky, nerdy and funny. I was innocent to worldly ways. My best friend taught me how to pick out nail polish colors and clothing. I didn't have a lot of money, but neither did she, so we paired well together.

It took me a total of five years to graduate from college, mostly because my first year up North was not accredited. I later had to repeat many of the classes. I attended summer college to make up some of the lost time. And I made it. On top of it all, I was able to overcome my social awkwardness and stilted upbringing. I had a boyfriend and he proposed to me my senior year of architecture. We had dated for some time. We both questioned the church. And we both had gone to public college together. We had a lot of our past in common.

Soothing Damages
I'm so glad I'm in the architecture profession. I truly enjoy it, and I am proud of my education. I have resorted to writing, art and sculpting, while raising my son. Church is not something we do. On occasion, we visit churches or other places of worship. Mostly, we live spiritually in our hearts. Our relationship with the Great Creator is our own. My marriage has been good. We have had our ups and downs, as most marriages do. But we have grown, and our bond is solid.
My son is the best gift of all. He wasn't even a part of my plan, but he sure does deserve the trophy in my life.

With my son, it was the ultimate promise to myself that I would break the chains that ran down through the family. I wanted to break the despair, the fear, the neglect, the abuse. I wanted to change things. I vowed never to touch him in anger, or an unhealthy or negative way. I vowed not to yell at him. I vowed to give him light, love and caring. I'm glad I was able to do this for him. I'm proud of that. He's never known any of the darkness that I knew in my childhood. I have never told him the stories that are now coming to light. But he's a young adult now and it is time for me to share my story.

41

AGE: THIRTEEN

BELOVED PATIENT

In came another patient, and another. I went into the golden-yellow waiting room and welcomed them. I usually had paperwork for them to fill out with a clipboard and pen. Then I would see if Dad's secretary or Mom needed anything else. I cleaned, filed or did mailings for her. Sometimes when they took breaks or had lunch, I would cash out the patients, schedule them for another visit and answer the phone. I took my job seriously.

Dad would be whistling a happy song in the back office; he was so happy at work. I would be smiling because Daddy was in a good mood. Then it struck me one day: He was always happy at work with his patients. It was at home that he became angry. It was a pattern. At that moment, I did not want to be his child; I wanted to be one of his beloved patients. I imagined him smiling at me and laughing with me; that would be incredible.

There was one patient left, so I went to the room and cleaned up after her. I had to clean with gloves, straighten and sanitize the entire room between patients, then wash my hands again. It was the routine when I was helping in Dad's office.

I would bring a patient with me and usher them to a room, explaining the procedure and providing robes before closing the door behind me. We gave them time to change, and Dad and the nurse/secretary went in for the exam. I took over at the front desk for the interim.

My pay was $1 per week and I only worked after school and during summer vacation. So, I figured it was fair. Plus, I was getting experience.

∼

42

AGE: THIRTEEN

Hopeless Determination

This Christmas had been a mistake as usual. Almost every major holiday was ruined by my dad's attitude and behavior. This Christmas was like any other. Our gifts to Daddy were not good enough; they lacked the love, attention to detail and quality that was demanded by our father.

The meal was never cooked correctly. One of the dishes always tasted wrong or was slightly burned or whatever. Mom usually ended up in tears at the table. Dad would leave the table yelling obscenities and go to his room, slamming the door. This would leave all of us children in tears staring at each other, trying to figure out what we had done wrong this time.

I made a pact that year with myself. I was going to make Daddy something handmade with love, that had detail and high quality. I was going to work on a cross-stitch pattern of a cabin in the mountains, much like our new home. It would be perfect. He could frame it. And he would be proud of it.

Mom found the kit for me. And I began working on it immediately. It was quite large, so it would take the whole year to make it. I didn't have much time to work on it with school, chores and my other activities. So every minute would count. Every cross-stitched thread that I placed, I thought I could make Daddy happy, make him feel loved.

The sun had rolled through the sky by day, the months rolled through time evenly and I found very little time for my project. By October, I still needed to finish half of it. I worked harder and longer, letting my piano and voice practice slip. I also allowed some of my homework to slip a little. This project would be completed on time.

I completed the cross-stitching the night of Christmas Eve. I vowed not to undertake such a huge project again for anyone. I was very lucky to have it done.

I finished in the nick of time. We opened gifts that same night – on Christmas Eve. Daddy opened his gifts last. My gift was at the bottom of the pile.

He complained about each gift as he opened them one by one. And then my gift was in his hands. This would change everything. He would feel loved. He would be happy. He would be proud. He had to be.

The paper was torn in a way that we could use it again and he pulled out my gift, holding it up and letting it fall open. The gentle scene of the cabin in the mountains was so beautiful.

"What am I going to do with this?" my Dad roared. "I don't want this."

And across the room, it went flying in slow motion. His

words were fixed in my head like a branding iron on skin. It had been hopeless determination on my part. I had thought he would see my love in every stroke of the needlework. I thought, for once, he would see me, love me.

Soothing Damages

My mother kept the piece for me and gave it to me years afterwards. I threw it away when no one was around. I had wanted the work of art to be timeless love, a barrier breaker, a father-daughter connector. He would never know. He would never understand.

I loved my father very much despite all the things that he did and all the things that he said. All I wanted was for him to love me back. As human beings, don't we all want to know that our parents loved us? Now that I look back in time, I think he did love me in his own way. It was just a strange way. He spoke through money and gifts, I believe. If he gave me a gift, he loved me. Those were rare times, and closely guarded.

43

AGE: THIRTEEN

Tarzan and Jane

A teenage boy from down the way was swinging on a vine, from alongside the road, out over the ravine. My family was in the car not far away waiting for my mom and dad to finish visiting with my aunt and uncle. My brother went over to the swinging vine and joined the mayhem. Then the teenage boy came over to the car and asked if I wanted to join them. My brother waved me over. I looked at the boy and decided I would be brave.

With both the boys giving me directions, I flew off the edge of the road and over the mountain side and over the valley. What a vivid rush of adrenaline. The trees were at their fullest; the forest was alive with adventure. It was a terrifyingly thrilling moment. And then I flew back toward the ledge by the road. I was so proud of myself. I flew into the arms of both boys. But I was only there for a moment and I couldn't seem to release the vine; my hands were clinging to this lifeline of nature. It was a large and heavy vine and it dragged me back off the ledge and swung me out over the ravine again. That's when my hands slid off and down I fell.

My brother estimated the fall was thirty feet. I landed in plump bushes at the bottom, breaking my fall. My body hurt all over, but I wasn't about to admit any pain. My pride moved me. When I stood on my two feet, that's when the pain kicked in. I had some real pain in my left ankle. The boys hoisted me up the cliff and onto the road.

Dad looked at my ankle and decided he wasn't sure if it was broken or not. He was a little perturbed, but I think he was genuinely worried about my ankle. He had my aunt take the rest of the family home while he drove me to the hospital forty minutes away, down the mountain.

We had a decent talk. I think he was surprised I would do such a thing, and I think he was impressed with my adventure.

The hospital took X-rays. I remember Daddy saying that I should be an X-ray technician because they made decent money and could work part time if they needed.

I thought to myself that I wanted nothing to do with the medical field; it was almost obligatory on everyone in our church. The aim of the church was to work in occupations that were in service to man.

I wanted to do something different. I wanted to choose a career that suited me and not my church.

The doctor and Daddy decided I had an acute sprained ankle and gave me crutches and a thick ankle bandage wrap.

I was proud to sport the crutches, it gave me an excuse to tell my story.

Not only was there a swinging vine involved, there was a boy in the story too. His name was Tarzan.

Soothing Damages

I think that on that day my father was focused and balanced mentally. He was my Dad, my real Dad. I have often wondered if looming bipolar tendencies worked to hide or accentuate the true spirit of this complex man.

44

AGE: FOURTEEN

Begging for Wishes

We were poor, or so I believed. I knew we were tight on money. Mom had an allowance for groceries every two weeks. It was tight. We very carefully went through the list of needs and figured out which ones we could afford and which ones we could not.

I had started my period at age twelve, and for two years had been using the free old-fashioned sanitary belt and pads that we received from the hospital. This was an elastic belt used to hold the non-adhesive pad in place. The pads were lumpy and leaky. When I went to boarding academy, the girls made fun of me. It seemed they all had the thinner adhesive pads and tampons. And in physical education class, you could see the pad clearly under my gym uniform. There was no swimming or wearing a bathing suit with a sanitary belt. If we went to the beach or swimming pool, I had to stand by myself out of the water in my shorts and tee shirt. I was so ashamed.

I needed tampons. But not only was this an issue of embarrassment, this was an issue of morals. There was a sexual stigma to tampons in my parents' generation. It all went back to church issues. They thought that if you wore tampons, you were more likely to have sex.

And so, I begged for a wish, a wish that may not and probably would not come true. I wished for tampons and adhesive napkins. Before confronting my mom, I prayed first about it. Did this act of desperation harken back to my rain prayer in elementary school? I don't know. Of course, Mom said she would have to ask Daddy.

Daddy's answer was a resounding "No." To him, there was no sense in it when we could get free pads from the hospital. That was that. I would have to find another way.

After some time, my adopted-aunt came to visit. She took me to the grocery store with her. We were passing through the feminine-hygiene aisle and she asked me if I needed anything from there. So, I told her my story. Her response was quiet and purposeful. She carefully pulled a few boxes off the shelf for me. She said we could pretend that they were for her if anyone asked. I couldn't believe it. I had been rescued.

Later, I started working as the chaplain's secretary and I started saving my own money for these items. Sometimes, if I didn't have enough money, my roommate and I would split a box. It worked.

Soothing Damages

Chapter 44

I remember that awful belt. Before and during boarding academy, every boy knew when I was on my period. It was the adults who didn't pay attention or pretended not to notice. I've looked at the launch dates of both the tampons and the adhesive pads; both were available on the market long before I needed them.

However, I really appreciated the new products that I bought. And I knew somehow, that if I could change this one thing in my life, I could change other things too with time.

We weren't poor either. My father obsessed about money. He grew up very poor and I believe that sometimes he went without meals when he was a kid because there weren't any to be had. I think he was trying not to let that happen to us and doing it the only way he knew how. He saved every penny.

My father controlled all the finances at home and at work. Everything was under lock and key. Even all the bank accounts were in his name. He didn't pay my mother when she worked for him. She had to beg for money for her own personal needs and for gas money. Mother discovered years later that he had paid off all his mortgages and was wanting us to believe that he was still in debt, but he was not.

He did have a weakness for cars. I don't know why or how he justified that in his mind. He was also willing to pay for a good education for me and my siblings. But everything else was all about saving a dollar.

∽

45

AGE: FIFTEEN

BOARDING SCHOOL FRIENDS

I had been sent to boarding school for my high school years. I stayed in a dormitory full of young women. There were around eighty or ninety of us. There was a boys' dorm across the campus. We were not allowed over there.

I picked a roommate who was in the same grade as me and we were both expected to get high grades. But when I met her, I knew it would work out flawlessly. Other friends we knew from grade school got a room next door to us. It was a perfect world. It was a school run by my church, so we all had the same rules and knew them.

Once every other month, we had a break from school. And what we would do was invite one to three friends home with us, or go to someone else's home. I suppose my parents wanted to see me, because they always opened their home to me and my friends. Daddy's blessing must have been on this, so this made me content as well. I usually invited a few friends to come home with me. Mom would come and pick us up. Daddy was less likely to fly into a rage when I had guests.

We would have the grandest time. We would all bunk in my room. If we kept quiet, we could stay up late talking and have a riot – at least for us it was. We would hike up and around the mountains through nature, and build forts in the woods or catch salamanders near the streams. We felt free and happy. My parents gave us some leeway, for which I was very thankful. Some of my best memories are bringing my buds home.

46

AGE: SIXTEEN

AROUND THE COUNTRY

Mom, my sister and I were taking the summer months to travel around the United States and into Canada in our Nissan 280ZX. I was sixteen, so I was driving and Mom had me drive most of the trip. I loved it. I felt free and alive. I stopped the car on the side of the road so many times just to take a picture with my new camera. So many beautiful places arose around each corner or over the next hill. It was stimulating and exciting. I drove through mountains, over bridges, and even onto a car ferry boat.

We traveled north from our beach condo in Florida and into the Carolinas. Then we meandered up and over into Montana where we visited some friends. Then we headed north into Calgary and Edmonton, Alberta, Canada, where we visited with relatives. I especially loved seeing the gorgeous Banff and Lake Louise. And on we went down into

Oregon and California, visiting friends at Yosemite National Park and family in Glendale. We toured through San Francisco and Los Angeles on our way to Phoenix, Arizona. We stepped on the four state corners plaque and then went on to see the Grand Canyon. After that I don't think we made too many stops; we mostly drove through long states. I think at that point we were tired and wanted to be home. What an amazing experience for the three of us together.

47

AGE: EIGHTEEN

WHORE

I had found the perfect gentleman in my boyfriend. He even asked me first if he could kiss me. He was truly amazing in every way. We went on great dates together. He always made me feel so special. I always wondered how I could be so happy with someone. We were just getting to know each other. We did encounter one problem and that was his car. He was on a strict budget and his car kept breaking down.

He drove a Toyota Celica hatchback. I remember it was white; it was a cute car. But it didn't like to function. Anyway, I had a curfew, a very inflexible one. Well, on one of our dates, his car decided to sputter and give out, putting us on the side of the road when we were supposed to be on the way back home to drop me off. This was before cell phones. We pushed the car up the road and into the closest gas station. Luckily, they had a pay phone there that I could use. While I was trying to find a quarter for the phone to call my parents, Alan tried to figure out what was wrong with the car.

I called home and had a couple minutes to explain before being cut off by the operator. I hoped my parents understood. My father had offered no help. It was all I could do. I went back to the car to check on Alan. Luckily, he had figured out what was wrong and was already fixing it, at least temporarily. I sat in the car with the door open while Alan finished fixing the car. I eyed my watch as time slowly crept past my deadline. I cringed. Dad was going to be upset and there was nothing I could do about it. My anxiety rose with expectations of what Daddy was going to say.

As soon as the car started, we were able to continue our journey to my home. Alan dropped me off at the front entrance of our condo and left. This was probably a wise decision. I went up the elevator and, as soon as I walked in, my dad got up and came straight for me. He put his hands around my shoulders and grabbed me hard. He yelled at me and pushed me around the room. My back finally hit the wall violently. I collapsed onto the floor. He picked me up and knocked me hard against the wall over and over, repeatedly calling me a whore.

Soothing Damages
That's the only word of the conversation that I remember. The rest of it was something about being late. I know they received my phone call. Dad chose to believe his own story and let me know that he thought the worst of me.

48

AGE: TWENTY THREE

WHITE CABINET

Alan and I married immediately after our graduation from college. We moved to Pittsburg, where I pursued my master's degree. Alan was hired as a mechanical engineer in the area. After I graduated, Alan received a job opportunity in Richmond, Virginia, and we accepted. We had bought our first home together, just north of the city in Mechanicsville. It was small, but nice, clean and comfortable.

My parents came up for a visit. They were going to give us a gift. But they wanted to assess the house first. After a good look around the property and the house, Daddy decided we needed a toolshed in the backyard for our yard equipment. That way we could park one of our cars in the garage. We really liked the idea, so I went shopping with my dad for the shed. We found a great little place that made them and delivered them for a reasonable price. We ordered a shed. It would be delivered in two weeks.

Back at home Dad decided I needed at least one cabinet in the garage for all my cleaners and related items. And we probably needed a few shelves around the garage to get stuff off the floor. My husband and Dad went and bought the black metal shelving. They came back and spent most of the day putting the shelves together, positioning them and loading them up, organizing. The next day, Daddy took me out to look for the cabinet. We found a nice fiberboard of white laminate. Dad and I spent the next day working on the cabinet. He was in a pretty good mood the whole day. We worked well together, and the cabinet came together slowly. We even made an extra trip to the hardware store to buy an extra shelf and put that into the cabinet as well. I think we were both proud and pleased with our efforts. It's one of my better memories of spending time with my dad. It was a nice visit overall from my parents. Dad may have been trying to make up for past times. He was on his good behavior. He may also have started seeing me as an adult. Maybe having my education out of the way, and having a solid job, gave me some respect.

Dad came and visited with my boss at work, making sure he was taking care of me. I worked at an electrical systems contractor's office. I designed fire alarm, nursing, security, and sound systems for buildings. Dad and my boss were both cut from the same cloth, so that went well. They even went to lunch together. My boss told me later that he really liked my dad.

Chapter 48

My dad and mom spent the next several days watching the squirrels and the birds in my backyard. It was a zoo out there, always bustling with life. And the squirrels were very entertaining. I think the squirrels knew that they had an audience and they did their best to entertain Mom and Dad.

49

AGE: THIRTY ONE TO THIRTY THREE

DAD'S FINAL PEACE

Daddy had diabetes. Apparently, he had it for years and it remained untreated. He denied he was ill. And despite all his due diligence, he passed away at the young age of sixty five. But of course, there were the complications first before his death.

His kidneys decided to stop working. Dialysis was his only choice. So, I moved down to Florida to be with my family and help with my father's health, even though I knew I had a young child in my arms and that Daddy would be a difficult patient. I left my husband up North and took my son, who was age two at the time. We made a home in a little apartment off US Highway 1 in the Melbourne area.

I would drop off my son with my mother. That way I would take Dad off her hands for the day. Sometimes I would let my sister take my son, so I could watch my father.

Chapter 49

The usual routine was to pick him up before lunch time and take him down to one of his favorite restaurants and eat with him. It was during one of these meals that he enlightened me about myself and all my family members.

He commented first about my mother. The good thing he said about her was that he always knew she would be a good mother to his children. I think I was in shock when he moved on to talk about my brother. Dad said that my brother was a waste of time and effort. I told him I didn't agree. But he didn't listen and moved on to me. I was uninteresting. I was predictable. I was boring. I never took chances. He had nothing nice to say about me. My younger sister however, was interesting and even exciting sometimes. Then he decided to talk about my husband. At that point I became livid. I was ready to pull my hair out and scream. I kept my mouth shut until we got into the van. I had never talked back to my father before that day. But that one day in history, I did. I told him exactly how I felt about what he had said. That we were all worth something. I told him that my husband was a good man, that mom deserved better and that my brother was a great person. He got silent, so very silent. I think I put him into shock. At least for a few minutes. Until we arrived at the dialysis center. Then after I wheeled Dad into the dialysis room, he told all the nurses and techs that I was treating him terribly and abusing him. He put on the act until we got back into the handicap van. He wouldn't look at me or speak to me after that.

Shortly after this incident, he was scheduled for his last possible dialysis access port to be placed. The surgery nurses let us in to see him before the procedure. He still had that attitude with me of not even looking at me or talking to me. I told him that I loved him. He didn't respond. That's how it ended with my father and me. He passed away in the hospital that night. I was thirty-three years old.

Soothing Damages
With my father, love was conditional, convenient, and temperamental. My mother taught us unconditional love. Thank goodness we had that.
I was always forgiving my father. And I forgave him this last time too. And I forgave him for everything. He was my father. I learned a lot of grief from my father, but I learned a lot of good things too. I learned how to be strong and my own form of a bad-ass. I stood up to my father. Who knew I could do that? And I withstood the test of time living as his child. I've become the person I've always wanted to be. And I have happiness in my life like I never knew.

∼

50

AGE: THIRTY FOUR

DADDY'S PRESENCE

We had Daddy's graveside memorial two days prior to Dad's visitation. I had been battling in my thoughts about the whole idea of it and my relationship with him. At my home the next morning, I woke and sat up in bed. There was a strong presence in the room. Someone was there. It was Daddy. But he was gone. No one was there; I didn't see anyone. It felt like Daddy. I didn't feel the usual fear or anxiety. I just felt a calmness. But it was Daddy. He was there to give me a message.

And suddenly my mind was full of love and understanding. Daddy was okay. He understood finally about all of us and everything. I had worried about his soul my whole lifetime. He was letting me know he was comfortable where he was and satisfied, that all would be well, and for me not to worry anymore. I felt that this was a personal message from him, that he finally understood me, that he truly felt loved by me and that he loved me.

I felt the need to tell my mom about the experience so that she would know what I had felt. I thought Daddy wanted me to extend the message to her at least. I believe she was content in the knowing and receiving it, and it may have helped her settle a few things as well.

Soothing Damages
That was the only time I felt my father's strong presence like that. It was an overwhelming experience, kind of like something washing over you.
I think I needed those feelings of closure and I'm very happy with the message that I received. I'm not sure what I experienced, but I believe it happened and I feel true to it.

51

AGE: THIRTY FIVE

HELP

I knew I needed help. I wasn't doing anyone any good, especially myself. I couldn't function well, couldn't feel happiness, and couldn't seem to move forward in a positive way. After I had been working with my doctors for several years, they diagnosed me with severe depression and anxiety. I decided to reach out and get some help. It was a difficult decision but one that I had to make for myself and those around me. I focused largely on my son who was a young child. He needed me.

I found a Christian rehab place that dealt with severe depression and anxiety. I decided to check myself in with the support of those who love me and support me. I needed and wanted to heal and become a better person. I stayed with the rehab center for a few months, working hard every day on spiritual, mental and physical self. It was tough. At least I was working toward a more positive me. That is what was important – that and the fact that I was worthy of this change.

We had personal therapy sessions at least once a day, along with group sessions once or twice a day on different topics. We had learning sessions on what tools are in our toolboxes on how to deal with anxiety and depression. These were informative. I never knew it was okay to feel angry or that it was okay to accept myself. I was not brought up that way.

I think one of the things that stood out to me was a story about standing in front of the Great Creator, and asking Him what He thought about me. He would look straight into my heart and see a worthy, beautiful person. So why couldn't I believe the same thing?

There was a family weekend when my family came to the center to try to begin to understand what I had been learning and how to help me along my way as my support team. They've each been so supportive ever since.

When it was time to come home, I was different, changed. I had goals, tools, and changes to make. I wanted to be a new person. It would take time, probably years, but I was stubborn enough that I would at the very least improve to reach new levels as a person. My family was thrilled to have me back home.

Soothing Damages

It's been many years since I was at the center. I still refer to it, and pull from the knowledge that they taught me. I think each year that I improve a little more. To this day, I still have a support team in place, and know that they are there for me. I think everyone needs this in their daily lives.

As far as reaching out for help, I believe that it's important to do that. Sometimes we need a special hand to help us over the rough patches. We cannot do everything by ourselves. I know I could not have made it without the help that I received from the center, the doctors and my friends and family.

52

AGE: THIRTY FIVE

After Help

The painful events of my lifetime are still vivid in my mind. I live with them as memories of my life and of who I am as a person. But I am proud and happy now. With help, I have processed and overcome so many negative scars, soothing the damages of my heart and soul.

Better and happier days eventually came into my life with time and therapy. I can write and talk about these incidents with bravery and understanding and forgiveness. There is no more pain. The pain has gone. There is a way for everyone to recover from their past. I hope I have demonstrated that it can be done. It's not easy. But it can be done. Start by believing in yourself and not giving into your past. Your past does not make your future. You make your future.

I looked for help because I wanted a future for myself. That's how it started. Then my desire for a whole life, grew. I wanted a future with my husband and my son and my family and friends. I wanted to be a complete person. I am still working on me.

Soothing Damages

I still suffer from medical issues that my doctors have been working on for years. We solve one issue, and it's on to the next. But I cannot complain. In every other aspect of my life, I am happy. I am blessed, loved, and treasured. I want these good blessings for you too. And may you have good health too.

53

AGE: THIRTY SEVEN

Mom

After getting help, I realized that Mom had been there the whole time and I asked myself where she had been. I understood that there had to be reasons for what happened, and that I needed to appreciate those details. I knew Mom was a good person, and that she was true to us children.

For a few years I struggled with anger and misunderstanding about my mom. Why hadn't she stopped Daddy from beating us? Why was she always standing on our side of the punishment line and not Daddy's? Didn't Mom have control too? And I had many other questions.

But as time passed, and I processed each of the events in my memory, I realized that Mom was a lot like us kids in a way. Daddy treated her like he treated us in many ways,

Chapter 53

especially making sure we were subordinate to his domineering attitude. I think Mom was afraid. She was afraid to test the line that was drawn in the sand, which was that Daddy didn't physically beat Mom. What if she did or said the wrong thing, would he cross that line? I think she feared Dad as much as we did, if not worse. She dealt with the bulk of his anger. And she acted as a buffer a lot of times for us kids, keeping us on the safe side of things.

If something needed to be told to Dad, Mom knew when and how best to give him the news. Sometimes it worked out and sometimes it didn't, but she was willing to take the risk for us children.

There was a lot of fear in the family. I know at least there was with me. And Mom had a lot of fear, too. Fear is what drove us. It forced our hand, our actions, our beliefs. It obliterated any love in the room.

We lived in a prison of fear. We had to appear right, whatever right was supposed to be. We had to hide our fear and act happy when other people were around. When the last guest left the house, the prison bars came smashing back down. Fear ran in my blood as I'm sure it did in my mother's.

Mom was an unconditionally loving mother to us children and to Daddy. He couldn't have asked for a better wife. She took great care of the family and his business. She did her very best in the situation that she found herself.

On a few occasions, Mom was going to divorce Dad, but found out that Daddy would fight for custody of us children. She decided that instead of getting the divorce to save herself; she would stay and save us kids from his wrath. If it wasn't for Mom, I'm not sure I would have been able to be saved from my deep dark pit of despair. Mom has been a hero in every way possible.

54

AGE: FIFTY

YOU ARE EXTRAORDINARY

I said it. Now make it so, by believing it. You are extraordinary.

Have you lived in the doghouse? Are you living in a doghouse now? Do you see your future in the doghouse? Are there spiderwebs? Is it raining? Do you have a dog who joins you in the doghouse?

All I'm saying is that each of us has a story. You have a story. And sometimes, it involves a doghouse. If it does, I want to reach out to you and say, "You are extraordinary." You can do amazing things for yourself. You can do amazing things for your life.

Let's stop the rain and push those clouds away. You can change your life and the lives of those around you, those of your family and friends, by taking one step at a time in the right direction. Walk toward the light. Let's let in the sunshine. Know that you can change your life. Believe it. Do it. Do not give up.

I say we get rid of the spiders, too. Once we believe in ourselves, we can start to set our boundaries. Anyone really negative in our lives – they are out. A little negative? Move them to your outer circle. Move people you trust into your inner circle. People who believe in you and build you up are the people you can put in your inner circle. Place your boundaries and stick with them.

And how about let's live in a real house with a roof that isn't leaky. Let's live in a house that is full of people who love us, care for us, support us and lift us up. Make your world. Create it. Make it yours. If you can believe this, you can do it. And how about we bring our pooch with us into that new life instead of living in his house. Imagine the difference it would make for him.

I see your life complete, satisfying, even happy. Do you know happy? Let me introduce you, here is happy. I think happy and you would get along great. Give it a try!

Chapter 54

Soothing Damages

No, I didn't do this overnight. When I was thirty-five, it took a few months to get my head around what my new plan was for my life. I had a son and I wanted a better life for him and myself. I would say to initially set up my real home and get out of the doghouse took me a year or two.

I'm fifty years old now. And I'm still working every day to make life better. But I feel like it's rolling along well now. Though, I never want to fall back into anything like before, not for me or anyone in my family. And I still have my battles, wars and down times. I have lots of scars to show my long story. I was a victim for so long, I didn't know what it meant to be anything else. I didn't know I could be different. I'm here to say that you can be. I think for some people it doesn't take very long. But for me, this has been my path; it was right for me. What is right for you is in front of you. You just need to start walking in the right direction. Get help. Move forward. Take life and make it yours.

I thought of myself as a slave, a servant, a subhuman being. I was molested, beaten, and broken in my youth. But where am I now? Who am I now? I, yes I, am extraordinary. I have walked the walk. I have brought in the sunlight, cast out the spiders in my life. I have made healthy boundaries, moved into a real home full of love and support, and brought my loved ones with me. If I can do this, so can you.

∽

APPENDIX I

Rudy's Activities, Ages: three to present

Classes from a liberal arts college:

- Piano – Ages: four to fourteen (master pianist / Piano Ensemble)
- Guitar – Ages: six to twelve
- Vocal/Choir – Ages: four to eighteen (soloist on occasions)
- Clarinet/Band – Ages: nine to eighteen (First Section-Third Chair / Wind Ensemble)
- Painting with Pastel, Acrylics, Watercolor – Ages: four to present (Master Pastel Artist)
- Photography – Ages: sixteen to seventeen, nineteen to twenty
- Sculpting – Ages: seven to eight
- Tennis – Ages: four to ten, sixteen to eighteen (two trophies)

- Swimming – Ages: three to eight, twenty to twenty-one (Swim Team)
- Drama – Ages: thirteen to eighteen (Ticket Box Office - Narrator / Little Drummer Boy – Star)

Summer Camp Courses:

- Horses
- Mini Motorbikes
- Lapidary
- Ceramics
- Swimming

Christian equivalent of Boy/Girl Scouts. Ages: twelve to fourteen. Earned more than fifty badges: Trees, Flowers, Shells, Birds, Butterflies, Music, Small Engines, Swimming, Braiding, Archery, Cooking, etc.

Hobbies: Ages three-present

- Reading
- Writing
- Sculpting
- Movies and TV Series
- Making Dollhouse Furniture
- Painting
- Making Wise Men
- Aerobics/True Barre

Playtime: Ages three to twelve

- Coloring
- Barbies
- Lite Brite
- Fisher Price Little People
- Bike-riding

APPENDIX II

Rudy's Home Rules from Memory, Ages: three to eighteen

My Rules:

1. Daddy was King. Serve Daddy first.
2. Big Brother was Prince. Serve him second.
3. Always look tidy/groomed.
4. Speak only when spoken to.
5. Play/work quietly, including music practice.
6. Homework, practice and chores done first after school and activities.
7. Forty five minutes piano practice daily.
8. Thirty minutes guitar practice daily.
9. Thirty minutes television daily, if time allowed.
10. Showered and in our pajamas.

11. When Daddy arrived at home, stay out of his sight unless called.
12. Friday night review of Weekly Memory Bible Verse and Study Guide Story.
13. Friday night, we watched Disney – if it didn't come on after sundown, the start of Sabbath.
14. Sabbath allowances when at home: coloring, Lite Brite, reading, sleeping. No swimming or playing.
15. Sunday extra chores assigned to each of us for the day: pulling weeds, picking up rotten oranges, tending the garden and Mom's flowers, giving the dog a bath, mowing the grass, etc.
16. Date the gentleman we present to you. Only date gentlemen that come from wealthy families. Don't date gentleman of a different color.

APPENDIX III

Church Rules from Memory, Ages: three to eighteen

1. Follow everything the Prophet says. It comes directly from God.
2. Follow your Bible.
3. Be a vegetarian. No eating meat or fish.
4. No using makeup.
5. No jewelry.
6. No dresses above the knee; no cleavage showing; shoulders always covered.
7. Bathing suits were to be one-piece and conservative.
8. Wednesday night Worship.
9. Friday night Worship.
10. Church-version of Girl/Boy Scouts for all children.

11. Go to a church elementary school, not public school.
12. Go to a church boarding academy, high school.
13. Go to a church college/university school. Learn to be a pastor, educator, doctor or nurse.
14. A woman's main job was to have children and raise them, not to have a real career.
15. Go to a church medical college/university for higher learning. Most people in this faith have medically related professions. Usually men were doctors, women were nurses.
16. Men were more important than women. Baby boys were desired more than baby girls.
17. Get married to someone in the same faith. Divorce is not allowed.
18. No wearing wedding rings or any kind of jewelry; that money should go to God in the offering plate.
19. No dancing.
20. No theatres, no going to the movies.
21. No alcohol, cigarettes, drugs, etc.
22. No cursing.
23. No working on Sabbath.
24. No swimming or playing on Sabbath.
25. Obey the Ten Commandments.
26. Anyone that was not from our church was not saved, so be careful who your friends are.
27. Sabbath activities included: Sabbath School, Church, Lunch, Lots of Outreach Ministries, Singing Together, Dinner, Evening Worship, Reading Prophet's Books or Bible, Sleep.
28. Leave the church or don't attend the church

schools; the church and even your "best friends" will disown/shun you.

Soothing Damages
I left this church when I was around the age of twenty-one and at a public state college. Most of my friends have disowned me because I have left the church. Recently I was passed over for being invited to a friend's funeral/memorial because of this.

I have come to a peaceful resolve about most of these issues. My thinking is that they were not truly friends from the beginning. Love can be fickle. I have made friends since and my circle of love and support is so much stronger and more supportive in its foundation.

Today, I understand that the church has relaxed its rules, and that the prophet is no longer the forerunner in the doctrines. This is good news.

ACKNOWLEDGMENTS

Thank you from my heart

To my husband, Doug, who absolutely has supported me in this endeavor.

To my bestie, Elizabeth, who has encouraged me along the way and read this book in advance for me.

To my mom, Natalie, who also pre-read this for me and supports the truth of the chronicles.

To my agent, Mary, who is uniquely a perfect fit for my book and me in every way.

ABOUT THE AUTHOR

Judith Villemain grew up in Orlando, Florida in her early years. Here she was exposed to music, sports, and education. During her teen years she lived in Highlands, North Carolina and went to boarding academy for her high school years in Candler, North Carolina.

In the mountains, she learned about nature and how to survive in one's environment. College followed at the University of Florida where she received her Bachelor's degree in Architectural Design. At this point she married her husband of twenty-seven years. She went on to gain her Master's in

Architecture from Carnegie Mellon University, where she specialized in Building Performance and Diagnostics. Acoustics and lighting were her favorite studies.

Judith worked in the architecture and building construction fields for several years before deciding to have a child. Her son changed her life, and she decided to be a stay-at-home mom. Now that her son is older, she spends her time painting watercolors and acrylics. She also sculpts goddess pendants and writes stories. Her hobbies include gaming, reading and movies. Sometimes, on an especially good day, she may make up a tune on the piano.

www.ingramcontent.com/pod-product-compliance
Lightning Source LLC
Chambersburg PA
CBHW052056110526
44591CB00013B/2237